Germaine Tillion was born in 1907, and after qualifying as an anthropologist spent the years between 1934 and 1940 (May) doing field work in the Aurès mountains of Algeria. In August 1940 she set up a resistance group, and in August 1942 was arrested by the Gestapo and sent to Ravensbrück concentration camp. After the war, she studied Nazi war crimes under the auspices of the Centre National de Recherche Scientifique. In 1954 she headed an inquiry for the Mendès-France government into educational provision in the then French colony of Algeria, and when the war of national liberation broke out she campaigned against the use of torture by French forces. In the course of a long anthropological career, she made twenty-one research trips to North Africa, eighteen of them to areas of nomadism, before becoming Director of Studies at the École Pratique des Hautes Études. In addition to the enormously successful *The Republic* of *Cousins*, now in its fifth edition, her publications include *Les ennemis complémentaires* (1958), *L'Afrique bascule vers l'avenir* (1959), and *Ravensbrück* (1973). Germaine Tillion lives part of the time in Paris, part in Brittany.

AL SAQI
BOOKS

Germaine Tillion

Al Saqi Books

Distributed by Zed Press

The Republic of Cousins

Women's Oppression in Mediterranean Society

Translated by Quintin Hoare

First published as
Le harem et les cousins
by Éditions du Seuil, Paris 1966
© Éditions du Seuil 1966

This edition first published 1983
© Al Saqi Books, 26 Westbourne Grove, London W2

Typeset by Comset Graphic Designs
Singapore

Printed in Great Britain by
The Thetford Press Ltd
Thetford, Norfolk

0 86356 100 4 Hb
0 86356 010 5 Pbk

CONTENTS

Concerning Ethnology—Preface to the Fourth Edition   9

1. **The Noble Mediterranean Peoples**   13

     Citizens and Brothers-in-law   13
     Between Horace and Antigone   16
     Socio-Analysis of the Harem   18
     Ethnography: a Sociology for External Use   21
     Interpretative Grids   22
     Conjuring Away Half the Human Race   24
     A Chronic Frustration   26
     Five Correlates   27
     The Ancient World   31

2. **From the Republic of Brothers-in-Law to the Republic of Cousins**   36

     A Place Where Incest Is Not Forbidden   36
     A Million Years of Political Argument   38
     Political Cross-Breeding and the Emergence
          of Intelligent Man   39
     The Palaeo-Political Age   45
     The Infant 'Civilization' Dandled on Bony Knees   48
     Were the Wives of Aurignacian Hunters Less Robust
          Than the Norman Women of Quebec?   50
     The Hundred Square Kilometres of a Palaeolithic
          Family   53

    Human Space, the Structures of Kinship, and
      Two Types of Natality   56
    The Neolithic 'Situation' Reproduces Certain Aspects
      of Man's Earliest State   57

3. **Keeping to Oneself**   61

    Incest and Nobility   61
    Prohibition of Exchange   63
    Kings of Egypt   65
    Patriarchs of Israel   68
    Indo-European Monarchs   70
    Keeping the Girls in the Family for the
      Boys in the Family   73
    Eating Meat From One's Herd Is Like Marrying a
      Paternal Uncle's Daughter   74

4. **The Maghreb in the Butter Age**   77

    In the Beginning Was a Continuation   77
    The Soup Civilization   78
    The Maghreb's First Ethnographer   81
    They Were Practising Circumcision a Thousand Years
      Before the Birth of the Prophet   82
    West of Egypt, an Almost Unknown Land   83
    Female Fashions, a Model of Constancy   86
    Headless Men and Dog-Headed Men   87
    A Huge Pile of Empty Shells   89
    Evergreen Foliage and Deciduous Roots   90
    Uncertain Jealousy   91

5. **'Lo, Our Wedding-Feast Is Come, O My Brother'** 93

    My Lord Brother   94
    'Don't Cry, Chapelon'   95
    The Honour of Sisters   98
    Manufacturing Jealousy   101
    Women, Like Fields, Are Part of the Patrimony   103
    'Our Son's A-marryin' a Furrin Girl!'   106
    Revolutions Come and Go, Mothers-in-law Remain 109

'Lo, Our Wedding-feast Is Come, O My Brother! Lo, the
    Day Is Come I Have So Longed For'   110
The 'Cousin/Brother' Is a Cousin/Husband   113

6. **Nobility According to Averroes and Nobility
    According to Ibn Khaldun**   116

Agriculturists and Nomads   116
Celtic 'Clan' and Berber 'Fraction'   118
Joint Honour   119
'No Man Knows What They Have in Their Hearts'   121
Two Orphans Go to Visit Their Mother   123
'Nobility and Honour Can Come Only From
    Absence of Mingling'   125
Ancestor Worship   127
'The Dunceboroughs Are Part of the Family, That's
    Why We Receive Them'   129
Golden Age   130
'Warn the Dummy Not to Drink All the Milk'   132
The Nomadic Clan   134

7. **Conflict With God**   136

A Selective Piety   136
The Veil According to St. Paul   137
Joan of Arc and Robert the Pious   138
Our Holy Mother Church Is a Masculine Mother   139
The Koranic Revolution   141
' ... Into Hell-fire and Shall Abide in It For Ever'   144
Matrilineal Descent and Orthodoxy   146
A Transfer Back to God, by Notarized Deed   148
The Geographical Distribution of the Veil
    Corresponds to Female Inheritance   149

8. **Bourgeois Snobbery**   151

Seven Thousand Years of Destroying the Old Structures   152
Divergences Between History and Ethnography   153
The Child-Devouring City   154

The Arrival of Adults Loaded Down With Convictions   156
Half-Way Through an Evolution   158
The Local Bigshot *Cha-t-Diya*: Neither the Worst
   Sheep Nor the Best   159
More Veiled Women in the Villages, Fewer in the Towns   161
A Case of Social Urticaria   163

9. **Women and the Veil**   166

The Last 'Colony'   166
'Whosoever Removes the Head-Dress or Kerchief...
   Shall Incur the Penalty'   167
On the Sea's Muslim Shore   171
The Ancient World, Beyond the Maghreb   174
The Influence of Invisible Women   174

Index   179

Concerning Ethnology

PREFACE TO THE FOURTH EDITION

Before publishing this book, I removed a number of rather technical chapters, partly to do more work on them and partly to avoid putting off my readers. That was exactly ten years ago and the chapters are still being worked on, while readers (more of them than I had expected, since a fourth edition is now on the way) frequently tell me they have been put off.

There is no doubt that this book, by virtue of its very subject-matter, belongs to a scientific no-man's-land—on the margins of history, prehistory, ethnology, and sociology—where it seeks to illuminate some more or less classic twilight zones. I can not, in this preface, summarize the work you are about to read, for it is already highly condensed—as condensed as I could make it without obscuring its attempted analyses and explanations. Let us simply say that it looks at History (the historical arena, the historical era, and even the historical air) through the prism of ethnology, so useful for educating us in the ways of the world.

Ethnology—not just a human science, but a humanism—occupies a position at the level of reciprocal knowledge among peoples comparable to that of dialogue at the individual level: a ceaseless two-way movement of thought, ceaselessly corrected. In dialogue, as in ethnology, there are two participants: an interlocutor (an unknown person, an unknown people) and, opposite, another being, the one you know both best and least. The dialogue gets under way, the shuttle flies to and fro, and each oscillation changes something—not just on one side, but on both: for what the interlocutor perceives about himself is what his partner does not see, and vice versa. But conversely, each sees in himself what the other fails to notice. The confrontation brings invisible *outlines* to the surface. It is something like the aerial reconnaissance of a landscape. You walk through the countryside and see a more or less twisting path, flanked by fields where wheat, oats, and rank weeds are growing; you notice a daisy, a clump of poppies, a little fieldmouse. From a plane or helicopter, you do not see the little fieldmouse or the daisy or the poppies; but in some field of sprouting oats you discern the pale outline of a perfect square, rectangle or circle—quite invisible when you have your nose in it or your feet upon it. When this geometric outline appears, you know it corresponds to something buried which has disturbed the plant growth: walls of a temple, a fortress, a palace or a house.

Everyday experience teaches each of us that every human being is born and grows up in a bubble, a little spherical universe, from whose shell the embyro we all are never entirely escapes. Through dialogue, we attempt such an escape, such a release, but release and escape remain very limited unless they scale the walls of those other universes represented by each culture, language, country, and religion—all of them fine enclosed gardens. Thus ethnology is first and foremost a dialogue with another culture. Then a questioning of oneself and the other. Then, if possible, a confrontation that goes beyond oneself and the other (let us not forget that it was only after the first ethnologists had undertaken such confrontations that the notion of the *unity* of the human race began to gain ground: a unity not just *physical*, but also *social*).

So one of my preliminary aims was to uncover the foundations of 'our' own society. But simply to define this society already constituted an unusual departure, since here it corresponds neither to a nation, nor to a language, nor to a religion, but exclusively to institutions, organizations, and structures—those operative among the so-called historical peoples. What is involved is most of Europe, half of Asia, and the north of Africa, together with their offshoots on the American continent. But what then remains outside a 'society' of such vast dimensions? Only the peoples we call 'savage'—in other words, those who still occupied a very large part of the earth's surface at the end of the fourteenth century but who now survive only in a few distant fastnesses that are game-preserves for crack anthropologists and objects of envy for *Clubs Méditerranée*.

Although the term 'savage' is no longer taken amiss, I prefer to call this type of society 'republic of brothers-in-law', to underline its most obvious feature, the obligation to marry non-kinsfolk—a device whose political, economic, and even biological implications have long ensured its members' survival. It could also be characterized by the expression 'zero growth', which is now coming back into fashion after a very long period of disrepute (indeed, I would guess that in Eurasia this period of disrepute began with the neolithic).

'Historical' society (our own) is called the 'republic of cousins' in this book. For it reveres its kin on the father's side, eschews that intensive socialization (known by the name 'exogamy') that preserved 'savage' society, and above all is an enthusiastic partisan of growth in every domain—economic, demographic, and territorial. This philosophy has served it well for a long time—so much so, that it has allowed it to eliminate the savage *respublica*. Indeed, mere contact between the two 'societies' seems everywhere to have been fatal to the weaker. For, though a number of crimes can indeed be laid at the door of the stronger, these are not enough to explain the collapses which contact has provoked. For that, it is apparently necessary to compare in depth the modes of operation and dominant tendencies of the two systems.

The conquering 'society' is the one in which all my readers and I myself (together with all our close and distant relatives, and all the people we know) are immersed. So it is not surprising if even the smallest identifiable disparity in its ways and customs immediately catches our eye, whereas its huge shared characteristics escape our attention (or appear to us as the result of a kind of intrinsic law of the species, or even a morality of supernatural origin). Over very many years, and in quite diverse areas and circumstances, I have had an opportunity to observe, compare, and even *see evolving* some of these 'characteristics', and they have seemed to me to concern directly some of our most dangerously pressing problems: the position of women and a kind of philosophy of growth.

We know that 'savage society' is widely dispersed across the globe. But the same is not true of the complex of institutions that characterize the 'republic of cousins', which for its part stretches and sprawls from Gibraltar to Japan, over a continuous territory with a very distinctive epicentre: the Mediterranean Levant. We find this diffusion radiating from a nucleus in the case of another phenomenon too—this time an economic one, directly related to a radical change in modes of production: the invention and dissemination of agriculture and stock-rearing, a gigantic material revolution (which can therefore be located and dated accurately at the dawn of the neolithic) that was also born east of the Mediterranean, spread from the Atlantic to the Pacific, and assumed the very dimensions of the 'republic of cousins'. My hypothesis is to connect the two: bread, butter, soup, and the cooking-pot with the origins of the harem, preferential marriage between cousins, and the philosophy of expansionism.[1]

Today the soup is dwindling in the cooking-pot, and it is no accident if the exigencies of the moment are bringing all the peoples of the historical zone to the brink of a reorientation: to replace expansionism by equilibrium and to calibrate growth in terms of resources. In so doing, they are all coming into conflict with modes of thought that arose (according to my hypothesis) at the very end of the stone age, and that for this very reason have penetrated all their philosophies so deeply that they have come to consider them sacred.

Paris, October 1974.

---

1. Careful scrutiny of a map of the distribution of the plough in the fifteenth century—one drawn by G.W. Hewes is reproduced on page 26 of Fernand Braudel's marvellous *Capitalism and Material Life* (London 1973)—will show that it roughly coincides with a similar map of the seclusion of women, which is not in the least surprising if my argument is accepted.

1
The Noble Mediterranean Peoples

*'For my part, I neither put entire faith
in this story...nor wholly disbelieve it.'*

HERODOTUS

I called this book The Republic of Cousins because I wanted to draw attention to a characteristic that sets traditional Mediterranean society off from modern societies and so-called savage societies alike. The fact that this characteristic seems to lie at the root of a persistent debasement of the female condition makes it interesting, and perhaps useful, to attempt to trace its distortions in time and in space.

If we divide the world into three sectors, each having its own structure, the modern sector may for obvious reasons be christened a 'republic of citizens'. As for so-called savage society, considerations with which anthropologists are familiar permit us to designate it a 'republic of brothers-in-law'.[1]

Citizens and Brothers-in-law

'Savage republics' and 'modern republics' both seem to be, if not logical, at least general features of human evolution. But the same

---

1. 'Primitive' societies are characterized by the fact that exogamy—the prohibition against marrying a legal kinswoman—is general. 'Legal' kinsfolk, in practice, comprise everybody bearing the same name and living on the same territory. One marriage partner will thus necessarily have to move away from home. This obligation (combined with a keen mistrust of younger or older relatives and in-laws) imposes on adults of both sexes the almost exclusive company of their brothers- and sisters-in-law (real or potential). See pp. 15 and 16 below.

may not be true of the Mediterranean structure, which has the distinction of possessing a geographical label and domain of its own: the two shores of the Mediterranean, with their hinterlands. The 'modern republic', on the other hand, can now be found in most parts of the globe and stretches from Peking to New York. The contrast between it and the scarcely more localized 'savage republic' is obvious, but since this little book is not much concerned with either of them, I need say no more about it.

There is no need to define the 'republic of citizens'. Everyone who knows how to read (and that perforce includes my readers) has attended a school in which, in the context of a lesson in civic rights and duties, some more or less adequate explanation of what a state, nation, or country is has been given. Everyone also knows that an important—for some even pre-eminent—solidarity unites them with other individuals belonging to the same national formation. The 'republic of citizens' is not all that young, but it is still putting down vigorous roots wherever the terrain favours it, and it is still extending its domain. It thrives in structured states, endowed with at least one big city and something more—such as a common language or religion, or at least an ancient dynasty. So considering that the entire globe is now divided into states, and that big cities are proliferating and growing, the 'republic of citizens' can be conceded to be a probably inevitable stage in human evolution. Is it the last? Many signs point to the emergence of vaster formations, not all of them derived from a political will, but rather the product of the needs of our epoch. And these formations are slowly infiltrating the popular consciousness of even the really old countries (nation-states). Simultaneously, however, new states are ensuring a revival of patriotism (though not perhaps of civic spirit) in its most juvenile forms.

Meanwhile, a survey of the world distribution of those societies which the eighteenth century termed 'savage' will readily show that even those that still survive are now effectively dying. It may be said of them that although their origins may be unknown, their destiny can be foretold. Even if the reading public rarely has any direct knowledge of these societies, it is increasingly interested in books about them.[2] The readers of such books have learnt that

---

2. It is not impossible that the frustrations imposed on us by modern society

customs which at first sight seem ridiculous, monstrous, or simply quaint often conceal a certain logic, and sometimes a certain wisdom.[3] Are they a very early stage, an 'infancy' of human society, preserved by chance in a few distant continents but elsewhere vanished? Many scholars have thought so, and many still do. Geographically, however, they can really be assigned only an approximate location. They seem to be represented above all in those regions not known to Greco-Latin antiquity; but it is impossible to assert that they did not once exist in the Mediterranean world as well, though in an epoch lit only by the faintest glimmers of protohistory.

Within these societies (which are, incidentally, as diverse as literate societies in the Middle Ages, and hence far more so than contemporary literate societies, which have a tendency towards uniformity), the most constant feature is the prohibition against marrying a woman bearing the same name as you, that is, who legally belongs to the same lineage. This means that in systems in which the name is transmitted by the father, one may not marry a cousin on the father's side, while in systems in which it is transmitted by the mother, all maternal cousins are considered as sisters and strictly forbidden—however distant the kinship may in fact be.

What this means in practice is that the boy will be unable to touch any of the women in the village or group of tents where he has been brought up, except in the deepest secrecy and at great risk, both natural and supernatural.[4] In 'foreign territory', however, there is another village or group of tents where he *must* choose a wife, and sometimes where he must go and settle for the rest of his life. The outcome of this situation is that a customary solidarity often unites the boy with his wife's brothers and cousins and with his sisters' husbands (in practice, little distinction is made among these, especially as the same term generally serves to denote both

---

may have contributed to this infatuation. At a more general level, the 'frustrations of evolution' will be one of the themes of this book.

3. This is what emerges from almost all contemporary ethnological studies. It has been most extensively and convincingly demonstrated by Claude Lévi-Strauss, in *The Savage Mind*, London 1966.

4. Systems also exist in which the child belongs to his mother's clan, but has to be brought up in his father's. In ethnographic jargon, the clan is then said to be at once matrilineal and patrilocal; this is precisely the case with the Tuareg, whom I shall be discussing in a study currently in preparation.

brothers and cousins). Which is why this kind of society may justifiably be called a 'republic of brothers-in-law'. Almost all anthropologists who have analysed exogamy since Margaret Mead's book first appeared quote the reply she received from the Arapesh when she questioned them about incest, and which she summarized as followed: 'Don't you want a brother-in-law? With whom will you hunt, with whom will you garden, whom will you go to visit?'[5]

Between Horace and Antigone

Any inhabitant of the Maghreb would reply to all these queries: 'I hunt and plant with the sons of my paternal uncles, with my cousins.' For there is a third structure, distinct from both the 'savage' one (of brothers-in-law) and the 'civilized' one (of citizens). This may be designated a 'republic of cousins', because the men who live in such a system consider their duties of solidarity with all relatives in the father's line to be more important than other obligations—including, very often, their civic or patriotic ones. Antigone, who put the duties she owed her dead brothers above her fatherland, is the model heroine for this type of society, and the approval the Ancients accorded her has not died with them. Horace, on the other hand, who cheerfully killed his brother-in-law in the name of the City, might serve as a hero for the 'republic of citizens'—though if the truth be told, in Mediterranean 'republics' a brother-in-law's life and a sister's happiness are held too cheap to have offered the young Roman any valid motive for inner conflict.[6] From this point of view, Horace is as characteristic of the region from which he sprang as Antigone, and the two of them mark two ideal frontiers of the 'republic of cousins': the pure Greek maiden its frontier with the fatherland, and the intrepid champion of Rome its border with the family.

The Mediterranean region, whence our two heroes sprang, for long was privileged. For long? We can be more precise, for this

---

5. Margaret Mead, *Sex and Temperament in Three Primitive Societies*, London 1935, p. 84.
6. See, in chapter 5, the section entitled 'The Honour of Sisters', p. 98 below.

geographical privilege was born contemporaneously with the present climate, and hence at the approximate moment that a particular sociological era was drawing to a close (the upper palaeolithic). It was maintained until goats, farmers, and pharaohs destroyed the finest forests of this earthly paradise and thus caused some of its springs to run dry. The fact is that the eastern shores of the Mediterranean, amid the luxuriant vegetation they had inherited from the previous era, gave birth to everything we subsume under the word 'civilization'. This event has been dubbed the 'neolithic revolution': it began about a hundred centuries ago. During the next twenty-five centuries, the inventions that were to change the face of the earth (agriculture, stock-rearing, haulage, navigation, weaving, pottery) spread like aureoles around their lightsource. Thanks to archaeology, it is possible to follow their tracks and thus to establish that the most ancient sediments by and large correspond to the Ancient World.[7]

Can a link be established between the structure here termed 'republic of cousins' and the geographical accident that—in a determinate place at a determinate time—afforded the human species such an extraordinary opportunity for achievement? In any case, such a link in no way means that agriculture can be associated in a general way with endogamy, but merely that in the Mediterranean zone a *particular endogamy* (that is, preferential marriage between the children of two brothers) was able to result from a *particular* social upheaval—whose origin must have been the great cultural event we have just mentioned. The Mediterranean endogamous structure is thus linked, not to an inevitable stage of human evolution, but to an event, or more precisely to a combination of circumstances. Each single event does indeed correspond to an evolutionary logic, but their conjunction constitutes a historical fact, with all the element of chance that this term implies. It goes without saying, moreover, that all this should be taken as conjecture rather than as a statement of fact.

---

7. It would be nice to be more specific, which is not impossible if the dates of the Levantine neolithic dispersal are properly established. Is this zone limited by the Danube, the Senegal, and the Ganges? Does it extend further? Not as far?

18

Socio-Analysis of the Harem

In the modern world, it so happens that the present occupants of this region are primarily Catholic or Orthodox Christians on the north side, mainly Muslims on the south.[8] It also happens that the seclusion of women, symbolized by the harem, has drawn world attention more to the latter area, to the sea's Muslim shore. It is from direct observation of the relevant societies that I have been led to postulate a causal relationship between tribal endogamy (or rather, its degenerate form) and a particular debasement of the female condition.

Debasement of the female condition is, in fact, a fairly general phenomenon in the world. Women are physically weaker than men, and it was both convenient and possible for a man to appropriate a woman, or even several women, and treat them as objects belonging to him (the reverse requires a very rare combination of circumstances). There are, consequently, many societies in which women are treated as beings devoid of reason. But the form of this bondage varies. In the Mediterranean zone, it assumes certain quite specific and extremely tenacious features, probably more tenacious than elsewhere because integrated into a coherent social system.

Thus the seclusion of Mediterranean women and the various forms of alienation to which they are subjected currently represent the most massive survival of human bondage. Furthermore, they do not just degrade the individual who is their victim or who benefits from them. They also, since no society is totally female or totally male, paralyse social evolution as a whole, and in the present-day competition between peoples constitute an irremediable source of retardation for those who have been unable to cast them off. Incidentally, this traditional degradation, affecting such a large number of individuals (half of society), does not enjoy male approval alone—since women, like slaves, are often complicit with

---

8. Significant Muslim minorities are also found north of the Mediterranean (Yugoslavia, Albania) significant Christian minorities to the south and east; there are also very ancient Jewish minorities in the various Muslim countries.

their servitude.[9] Moreover, its enemies are not all female. But just as no milieu exists in which views limited exclusively to women or exclusively to men can be found,[10] so there nowhere exists an insulated misfortune that is solely feminine, nor an abasement that afflicts daughters without miring their fathers, or mothers without marking their sons. Moreover, through childhood, the overall diminution of woman's role and value as a human being—beyond individual misery—is transmitted to society as a whole and acts as a brake upon it.

For all these reasons, I felt it would be useful *now* to explain, or (to use a fashionable neologism) 'demystify', the harem. The present study will thus offer not a description of the harem, but an attempt to track down its sources and then, once these have been identified, to present an analysis—a 'socio-analysis'—of them. Just like a psychoanalyst, in fact, we shall first have to observe closely the subject that concerns us—a contemporary, or almost contemporary, society—and then attach great importance to its mistakes or 'slips'.[11] Subsequently, to explain these we shall have, with its own help, to decode its dreams and delve into its most distant past, right to its earliest infancy. Like the psychoanalyst, we shall thus avail ourselves of two sources of information: on the one hand, behaviour patterns, present and verifiable; on the other, comparison of these with memories, nightmares, and obsessions. In practice, the two lines of inquiry proceed in step, each impelling the other forward.

When the elements of this whole—that constituted by my own observation—were assembled, a number of conclusions emerged that warranted hypotheses. These seem fairly solid to me, but they

---

9. A Swiss journalist told me of a very active women's association in his country whose aim was to *oppose* female suffrage.

10. One can find views espoused, for instance, by 55 per cent of women and 45 per cent of men, but analysis goes no further. Even in those countries in which they have extensive rights, however, women have not had the same higher education as men and do not pursue the same careers, at least statistically.

11. It is the aberrant, maverick facts that, in sociology, play the revelatory role that psychoanalysis attributes to 'slips'. See, in this connection, all the practices found among Muslims that conflict with Islam: e.g. pp. 29-30 and pp. 82 ff. below.

require an immense step back in time. And this in turn led me to formulate another series of hypotheses, regarding the very distant roots of human society. Unfortunately, the second series of hypotheses—the less solid—is located right at the beginning of the book. It was not without misgivings, however, that in presenting my conclusions I adopted the reverse order to that followed in my research.

The book was in fact entirely thought out and written starting with the last chapters: in other words, with a very careful study of contemporary phenomena, contemporary societies, and *societal transformations* occurring in the present century. Subsequently, in seeking the links that bound them and the nature of the forces that maintained them from century to century, I was led to go right back to prehistoric times. Thus, by here following the chronological order of history, I have done violence to the logical order of reflection. I have done so for the sake of clarity, since it is genuinely difficult to set out a tangled history by beginning at the end. Nonetheless, as we all know, events must run their course before becoming history, so that all true history exists only by virtue of its conclusion, and begins its historical career from there.

Keeping, in short, to the normal chronological order, in the three following chapters I have grouped all the facts of a historical and even prehistorical nature to which I refer. From these I draw hypotheses that do not constitute necessary foundations for the following chapters, but in my view illuminate them. I would like this first part, which might be entitled 'Ethnology over Time', to be seen as a kind of scaffolding, useful in affording a bird's-eye view of the vast prospect of centuries whose presence—behind the widely scattered and highly topical social facts that will be described in the remainder of this study—we shall thereafter continually have to assume. The term 'scaffolding' implies a 'provisional structure'— which means that I have no intention of defending the solidarity of this first series of hypotheses. On the other hand, I think that their location can be accepted and the very distant origin of the various social phenomena studied here conceded. For it is certainly at the end of prehistory that we must situate, not the beginning of the 'harem', but the beginning of the processes that was to culminate in it. Our scaffolding will be useful, too, insofar as it forces us to conceptualize the here and now in the light of a very distant past.

Ethnography: a Sociology for External Use

A little over a century ago, when the human sciences began their career, ethnography might have been defined as 'external sociology' or the sociology of others. Since then, however, this 'sociology for external use' has greatly facilitated knowledge of our own societies, since from the outset it required a move outside our habitual surroundings, in other words a serene and lucid stance. The 'savages' of the New Worlds monopolized the attention of four generations of anthropologists, and thus stimulated a decisive advance in the knowledge of our species as such. But they allowed all the human sciences to become sciences only because they stripped them of their innocence from the start, forcing them out of their habitual surroundings. It is, moreover, symptomatic in this regard that the only such intellectual sortie outside habitual surroundings effected before the nineteenth century—classical studies—was accorded the noble title 'humanities'.

But our purpose here is to study deeply rooted customs appertaining to those my friend Marcel Griaule used ironically to term the 'noble Mediterranean peoples'.[12] From our chosen vantage-point, moreover, the difference between Muslim, Jew and Christian is slight—we are dealing with 'our' society, 'our' civilization. That is why it is useful to begin by clambering up a pyramid of centuries, to afford ourselves here at home the bird's-eye view which the outsider enjoys. Despite all these excellent reasons, proceeding from the unknown to the known represents a first serious lapse from the austere ethnographic virtue that was—and still remains—my ideal. It will unfortunately not be the only one, for this book is almost exactly the opposite of what I should like to produce.

The remainder of this study is devoted to observation of a certain so-called tribal society and analysis of its principal idiosyncrasies.[13] It will sometimes take us outside the Maghreb, but in the main will lead us to all corners of that subcontinent. Since the latter is huge

---

12. Marcel Griaule, *Méthodes de l'ethnographie*, Paris 1957, p. 4.
13. For some years now, ethnologists have used the methods of ethnography to investigate their own societies. For example, L. Bernot and R. Blancard, *Nouville, un village français*, Paris 1953; Pierre Bourdieu, *Célibat et condition paysanne dans le Béarn*, Paris 1962.

and diverse, we shall be obliged to visit it in the guise of ethnologists more than ethnographers—though I have always wanted to be more of an ethnographer than an ethnologist.[14] In the final chapter, entitled 'Women and the Veil', some conclusions will be found. The main one consists of linking the seclusion of women throughout the Mediterranean basin to *the evolution and ceaseless degeneration of tribal society*. The reasons why this degraded position has so often been wrongly attributed to Islam will also be found there. Lastly, a very brief description will be given of the damage it wreaks.

Interpretative Grids

It was because of this third part that I decided to publish the study without waiting until I could furnish the scholarly apparatus with which I should have liked to equip it. For I felt that its publication could be useful *now*. This, then, is one of the reasons why the specialist reader will perhaps be surprised to find only a simplified version of the learned paraphernalia in which sociology is normally accoutred.[15]

I have also striven to use the most everyday language. Today, the vast development of all the sciences imposes a specialization that is logically bound to grow still further. However, for several generations now it has not allowed anyone to inventory the entirety of the intellectual capital at the disposal of our species; and even professional scientists accept that they will know little or nothing of those fields that do not fall precisely within their own speciality. But there are certain specialities that concern all the earth's inhabitants, and from time to time a great disaster occurs which faces everybody with the same inexorable questions.

---

14. See pp. 23–4 below.
15. Furthermore, I should have liked to choose the quotations I give with greater care, but (like all people who do not know how to safeguard their time) I find it almost impossible to write in Paris, where I have my books. So it was while on vacation, ill, or travelling that I composed the bulk of this study: in trains, ships, cafés, hotels, under a tent or a shady tree, for the most part with only my not-very-good memory as a library.

In particular, it is by now almost a cliché to speak of the global danger represented by the prospects of world demography. Yet even so, not enough is said about it, since nothing that might begin to embody a remedy has been undertaken, or even identified. A certain politician referred in 1965 to the total amount of aid to the underdeveloped countries, which he put at 5,000 million dollars.[16] At the same time, he estimated at 10,000 million dollars the quantity of aid required simply *to prevent poverty from increasing*—in other words, to compensate for the impoverishment caused by the huge population growth. This means that not only are poor people poorer with each passing day, but they are also more and more numerous. If it is possible to cure the world's disease at present, how will it be cured when it has doubled? For it will have doubled twice over: doubled in seriousness for each individual affected, and affecting twice as many individuals. This study is concerned neither with economics nor with demography. It does, however, seek to throw light on a certain axis of our evolution: *the axis responsible for current demographic realities*.[17] It thus also locates itself within a practical world perspective.

In addition, everyone who writes obviously has motives for doing so. These vary from person to person, but are always connected with the most private dimension of individual experience. So far as I am concerned, I have an opportunity, from two different angles, to gauge men's disarray before the world they have made, and twice to see the real support an understanding—in other words, an analysis—of crushing mechanisms can afford to those being crushed (besides, this light thrown on monsters is also, I am sure, one effective way of exorcizing them). For ethnography, unlike the other human sciences, is not satisfied with archives, statistics, and secondary sources: the ethnographer must interrogate living human beings, not texts. As a consequence, he must also reply to questions, offer explanations and self-explanations, and, if he wishes really to understand, must first make sure he is really understood. In a word,

---

16. Jules Moch, *L'adaptation de l'ONU au monde d'aujourd'hui*, Paris 1965, pp. 149-50. [Note to 1974 edition: The oil crisis has offered some so-called underdeveloped countries a reprieve, but it has not solved all their problems.]
17. See pp. 51-6 below.

I would say that ethnography and ethnology (in practice these are hard to separate[18]) are reflexive, reciprocal sciences, in which misfortune is viewed at close quarters, but in which 'human reality' is interpreted in all its originality, wealth, and intimacy only through the fine grid of lived experience. Each of us possesses this 'interpretative grid', whose mesh is progressively reduced throughout our lives. The mesh of mine was reduced between 1940 and 1945, in the fraternity of great danger, with people whose origins and cultural formation were very disparate, but who all really wanted to understand: people who were enduring things that were very hard to endure and wanted to know why. Once they had understood, in their innermost hearts, a little mechanism called reason began to operate again; and this often, quite miraculously, set in motion the delicate gears that anatomists and doctors study, which Xavier Bichat used to call 'the complex of functions that resist death'.[19]

In short, my profession and my life have taught me that although not all intelligent people are necessarily educated (nor, for that matter, are educated people necessarily intelligent), all intelligent people deserve to be consulted about matters that concern them. And the problem studied in the following pages—the degraded condition of women in the Mediterranean zone—very directly concerns the destiny of part of the human race. Or rather, the destiny of us all, since it is by now unthinkable that a significant fraction of humanity could evolve in isolation.

Conjuring Away Half the Human Race

In the early sixties, when I was unearthing the data for this study,[20] the absence of women from all public places was still a source of

18. The ethnographer studies and describes populations directly; the ethnologist compares ethnographical studies with one another, and reflects upon them in order to draw conclusions; the anthropologist tries to situate the whole within the perspective of a history of Mankind. In practice, it is not possible to observe well without reflecting, or to reflect well without observing.

19. Xavier Bichat, *Recherches physiologiques sur la vie et sur la mort*, Paris 1800.

20. See note 32 below.

amazement for the traveller visiting the countries surrounding the Mediterranean. Yet almost all those countries are administered today by modern governments, aware of the danger, which vie with each other in passing laws aimed at involving the female half of the population in national life. In vain. Resistance from the environment remains perpetually stronger than the law. What does this resistance stem from? Where is it to be located? This will be my real subject.

Many people believe that this stubborn resistance derives originally from the Muslim religion, certainly very widespread in the area of the world where female society is most separate from that of men. They believe this all the more readily because, in all countries, a tendency exists to consider everything related to old family customs as sacred, hence religious. Muslim peasants are no exception to this rule, and in all good faith corroborate an opinion against which educated Muslims protest in vain. It will be enough, however, for us to locate the segregation of women accurately in time and space, and we shall at once see that the zone that corresponds to it geographically covers an area whose frontiers are not those of the Muslim religion. For it is *still necessary today* to include the entire Christian shore of the Mediterranean,[21] while on the other hand it is necessary to exclude huge regions converted to Islam very early. Historically, any sortie into the past likewise shows us that harem and veil are infinitely more ancient than the revelation of the Koran.[22] Moreover, the lack of either geographical or historical correspondence between the harem's area of distribution and the Muslim religion is not the only significant index. For, as we shall see, an analysis of institutions likewise rules

---

21. Without forgetting the areas conquered by its inhabitants, notably certain regions of the American continent: Texas, Mexico, and South America.

22. 'There is possibly a reference to the former [the veil] in an inscription of Rameses III at Medinet Habu .... women wearing veils on their heads like those worn by the modern peasant women in many parts of Egypt occur several times in those reliefs in the tomb of Petosiris that are executed in Greek style.' W.S. Blackman, *The Fellahin of Upper Egypt*, London 1927, pp. 285-6. The Greek gynaeceum was a harem.

out any religious origin for the effacement of women in the Mediterranean basin.[23]

The view that attributes the origin of the harem and the veil to Islam by no means excludes, on the part of those who peddle it, countless anecdotes about an overdevelopment of male jealousy simultaneously seen as one explanation of the phenomenon. Jealousy is thus, somewhat oddly, associated with religious faith. Yet it is as hard to imagine a jealousy derived from religion as a religion derived from jealousy. Must we then attribute veil and harem to a specific climate, or a specific race? We shall see that this too is inconsistent with everything we know of the past.[24] So what is the reason for this stubborn survival, which to this day, wherever it flourishes, constitutes the most serious obstacle to progress?

A Chronic Frustration

The hypotheses I am putting forward are based on direct observation of semi-nomadic tribes whose life I shared for many years, long enough to see the people who belonged to them evolve. And it is not, in fact, in institutions, but in the way these too evolve, that I believe I can discern a contradiction,—or as psychiatrists say, a conflict. And the 'solitary confinement' of women seems to me to result very directly from this conflict. Just like the psychological complexes that Freudians study in individuals, the 'conflict' in question appears to be the product of a chronic 'frustration', a habitual 'aggression', to which the organism—here society—responds by a 'defensive reaction'. As is well known, there is a persuasive medical theory according to which a 'defensive reaction' of this kind in the physical domain is the root cause of urticaria (hives), asthma, and so-called allergic illnesses in general.[25] The people who suffer from such illnesses know equally well that they can be far more unbearable and dangerous than the attacks (tobacco, dust) that provoke them. The social allergy to which I am refer-

---

23. See chapter 7, 'Conflict with God'.
24. See, in chapter 4, the section entitled 'Uncertain Jealousy', p. 91.
25. See chapter 9, 'Women and the Veil'.

ring is still active, since I have observed it myself. But its beginnings are already visible at the brink of prehistory's vast shadows.

The better to underline certain of the forms of internal and external aggression to which the society we are examining was subjected over the centuries, we need to look at five pairs of correlates. These are ancient, but still normal throughout North Africa; they may also be found in the Arab world, among Christians and Muslims alike; and they even stretch beyond the frontiers of the latter. The relationships may at first sight seem incongruous, but they are welded together by a constant pairing, too constant certainly to be explained by chance. Is there some logic that welds our pairs of correlates together two by two, like the blades of certain propellers? And that subsequently, like a propeller-shaft, also welds all those pairs of fins together? Those who have a visual imagination may amuse themselves by sketching the whole thing, along the lines of an engine like that which powers some aeroplanes. The originality of our engine lies in the fact that it runs in reverse, and instead of pulling the societies it has in tow forwards to the future, to the unknown, it drags them back towards a dead past.

Five Correlates

First Correlate: the Veil and the City

The veil of women in the Maghreb is related to urbanization. In other words, Muslim women wear the veil only when they live in a town, while country women go about with their faces uncovered. This correlate, standard throughout the Maghreb and the Arab world, is well known.[26] The new factor, however, which has not I think yet been pointed out, is that though the veil is now on the decline in the cities, it is compensating for this with an advance in the villages. I have known women in small towns in Morocco or the Constantinois who started wearing it less than ten years ago; in the Oran region, country women who did not veil themselves to go into

---

26. Among certain Mediterranean Christians and traditionalist Jews, though women are not veiled, they are shut up until old age and murdered in the event of adultery (or suspicion of adultery).

town twenty years ago do so today; in Mauritania, where urbanization is very recent, the same regrettable trend can be discerned.

Second Correlate: Nobility and Endogamy
For the inhabitants of the Maghreb, nobility is related to marriage between cousins in the paternal line. The more noble one is, the stricter the obligation will be. Or rather, the more endogamous the family to which one belongs is, the more noble one will be. At first sight, this kind of pride may appear like a familial 'racism'—but that would be jumping to conclusions. For if that were really the case, the agnatic group would tolerate a son's marriage to a woman from outside less easily than a daughter's marriage to a man from outside (where the family blood is lost, but not mixed). In fact, however, the reverse is the case, at least in rural areas, where it was considered shameful less than ten years ago for a big family to marry its daughters to outsiders, whereas misalliances between sons and outside women could apparently be accepted.[27] If this twin reaction were a modern phenomenon, it might be possible to explain it by familiarity, because of the frequency nowadays of marriages between young male heirs from the Maghreb and Christian girls they have met as students at university.[28] But this is not at all the case: the twin reaction actually seems to be archaic, while the spread of mixed marriages is very recent.

Third Correlate: North of the Sahara, Women Inherit Wherever the Tribe Is Destroyed
The relationship between inheritance by women and the destruction of sedentary tribes can easily be explained, since it is female inheritance that destroys the tribe. The entire tribal structure rests on the impossibility for anyone outside the ancestor's lineage to own land belonging to the familial patrimony. To keep such land intact

---

27. I have seen this personally, especially in the Constantine region, in rural areas of Morocco, and among the nomads of Mauritania. In the town of Tlemcen, by contrast, families refuse point-blank to marry sons to girls who do not belong to the local bourgeoisie, whereas daughters may just possibly marry rich outsiders. Naturally, more and more young people are refusing to submit. (We may note that in Tlemcen we are in a typically urban milieu, strongly influenced by its Turkish bourgeoisie.)

28. Permitted marriages according to the Koran, whereas marriage between a Muslim girl and a Christian boy poses a religious problem.

it is thus necessary not only to forbid its sale to outsiders—this goes without saying, and occurs in many countries—but also to have a system of inheritance so designed that no outsider can legally become an heir. Now, when a daughter marries a man who is not her cousin in the paternal line, the children born of this marriage belong legally to their father's family and are thus outsiders to the lineage of their maternal grandfather. If, in accordance with the prescriptions of the Koran, the daughter then inherits from her father the half-share that is her right, she will transmit this part of the patrimony to her children, which means to outsiders. To guard against that danger, the inhabitants of the Maghreb have combined the two possible systems of protection: to disinherit all daughters (which means violating the law of the Koran) and to marry them systematically to relatives in the paternal line. Only the former procedure, of course, is always effective, and wherever it has not been applied the tribe has ceased to exist.

Fourth Correlate: Destruction of the Tribe Coincides With Piety
This may easily be deduced as a consequence of the foregoing correlate.[29] For, in Islam, destruction of the tribe is directly related to religious observance, since Koranic law requires that all sons inherit a share of the father's property and all daughters a half-share. Religious law is thus doubly lethal to tribal structures. If one wishes to preserve a large patrimony over centuries, it is helpful indeed to privilege a single heir, a practice that is not in conformity with the Koran and has apparently disappeared throughout the Maghreb (though vestiges of it survive almost everywhere there).[30] It is even more vital not to allow an outsider to own an enclave in the patrimonial domain—which, as we have seen, excludes a daughter's children from their maternal grandfather's inheritance. This latter practice, which blatantly violates the prescriptions of the Koran, is still customary in many, though not all, regions of North Africa. For in the course of their conversion to Islam, the peasant tribes of North Africa found themselves faced with a most cruel dilemma:

---

29. Piety inexorably destroys the tribe; but it is also possible that destruction of the tribe, and the consequent loss of honour, stimulate piety as a compensation.
30. In connection with this, see the special position of the eldest son in the Mediterranean area: chapter 5, section entitled 'My Lord Brother', p. 94.

either they could apply the law of the prophet—in which case the tribe would be smashed—or they could save the tribe, but only *by violating religious law.* The fact that so many tribes have survived throughout the Maghreb is sufficient proof of the choice that was made, and also puts 'Muslim fanaticism' into its proper perspective. In any case, it all seems as if the Koranic lawgiver—right back in the seventh century—deliberately used inheritance in both lines (male and female) to pulverize the tribal system, and thus to equalize, modernize, revolutionize, and democratize Arab society.[31]

Fifth Correlate: North of the Sahara, Daughters are Veiled Only Where They can Inherit
Here we have a strange (and constant) phenomenon, for all the world as if women lost control of their own persons when they acquired rights over their father's inheritance, in other words, when they gained some economic power. One might seek to explain this anomaly as the consequence of some religious fervour which, after destroying the tribe through the imposition of female inheritance, also brought the veil and the harem into esteem. I do not think this explanation should be entirely ruled out, for in all countries genuine and enlightened piety brings bigotry (attachment to forms held to be religious) in its wake. But a much more likely hypothesis is that we are dealing with a causal sequence which I have observed personally: 1. religious fervour imposes female inheritance; 2. female inheritance destroys the tribe; 3. the destroyed tribe accepts outsiders; 4. fathers then veil their daughters, *to preserve them for the boys of the family notwithstanding.*

Since Morocco became independent, Koranic law has become obligatory in the countryside, which constitutes a novel, revolutionary fact of great sociological import. In the case of independent Algeria, no one yet knows how things are really going to turn out. Yet it is noteworthy that in both countries peasant inheritance is tending to dwindle to the point where it no longer allows families to

---

31. Democratize, but not 'socialize': for the Koran, if all its prescriptions regarding inheritance are followed, pulverizes private property but without negating or destroying it. See Maxime Rodinson, *Islam and Capitalism*, Harmondsworth 1977.

live off the exploitation of their ancestral domains alone; and this circumstance is going to facilitate the virtues of detachment that religious law and Marxist civic spirit alike now require of Maghreb landowners. (I venture to associate these two influences, because in practice they are collaborating in the destruction of hereditary landholdings.)

If this perspective is accepted, then we are dealing—within an area that remains to be defined but does not correspond to religious frontiers—with a society that has suffered from a permanent internal aggression since early antiquity and has reacted against it clumsily.

Before tackling the contemporary aspects of this twin mechanism (aggression and defence), we must first at least pose, if not answer, certain questions about its origins.

The Ancient World

Certain theoretical aspects of this study go far beyond the boundaries of Africa. Their point of departure, however, is direct observation: my own field work, which from 1934 to the present has led me to roam far and wide over the subcontinent Arabs call the *Maghreb*. The word means 'setting sun', and conveniently designates a homogeneous geographical zone and civilization whose boundaries are somewhat ill-defined. Let us take them here to incorporate, west of Egypt, all the peoples of Africa whose language and culture are Berber-Arab: in other words, five states starting from the Atlantic in the west—Mauritania, Morocco, Algeria, Tunisia, and Libya—to which should be added northern Niger and northern Mali. As for Egypt itself, politically and ethnographically it forms the backbone of the great Arab bird, the border country in which the two contrary currents of Maghreb and Levant meet. The Ancients attached it to Asia, and placed the outermost limit of Africa on the present Libyan frontier. That corresponds to a very old and still operative sociological reality.

I have had the chance to observe most of the things about which I am speaking on the scene, over a long period.[32] This means that I

---

32. Some ten years in the field, less than two in cities, and the rest of the time among peasants and nomads. I spoke the dialect of the Shawiya Berbers. My first

32

shall not use categories of social facts without taking account of their environment—which is familiar to me. I know the so-called archaic regions best, those peopled by sedentary or semi-nomadic peasants. But I have also lived among nomads speaking Berber; among nomads speaking Arabic; among peasants who have become agricultural labourers, workers, soldiers, or tradesmen; and, of course, among town-dwellers. Between these various social categories, there are numerous points of similarity and dissimilarity, some of them very ancient and others recent. But it is possible to differentiate them only when one knows Maghreb society as a whole fairly well.

Some of the features dealt with in this study can also be encountered in the conservative sectors of a still vaster zone than the Maghreb subcontinent. This area corresponds to the domain of the Semitic: it thus extends, beneath the Levantine wing of the Arab bird, all the way to the Indian Ocean. I have travelled there, but will not refer to so superficial a knowledge without basing it on texts; with the support of these, however, I shall be able to compare a social residue discovered in the Maghreb—common to all the Berber groups and visibly anterior to Islam—with analogous survivals coming from the Semitic areas of the Middle East. The Berber residue in question does indeed seem to me to have no connection with Islam, but this does not mean it has none with Arabism. The Muslim Arabs who invaded North Africa were not, of course, all doctors in theology; so they might have exerted a non-Muslim influence on the countries they conquered. But it was

scientific expeditions (1934–37) were sponsored by the International African Institute; the ones that followed (1939–40, 1964–65 and 1965–66) by the Centre National de la Recherche Scientifique. I take this opportunity to thank them, and also the École Pratique des Hautes Études, the Ministère de l'Éducation Nationale and the World Health Organization, who allowed me to make numerous research trips in between the full-scale expeditions. It was, in fact, the WHO that suggested that in 1961 I carry out an investigation on its behalf, covering the entire Middle East (Egypt, Pakistan, Iran, Iraq, Lebanon, Syria, Jordan, and Israel), with a brief to pay special attention to the position of women there. In the course of that rapid journey, I came to the conclusion that it was impossible to speak usefully about the situation without explaining it; that one could not explain it without going back a very long way; but that to do this would be to perform a great service. Such was the origin of the present study.

above all through the medium of their faith that they influenced the old conservative Maghreb, which still speaks Berber today.

Another argument militates in favour of the very great antiquity of this residue common to Berbers and Arabs, and that is its diffusion: it overspills their own domain, covers the Semitic area and even stretches far beyond it. Moreover, it affects what is most essential, and hence most original (in both senses), in a society, though this latter argument is less convincing, in my view, than the preceding one.[33] At all events, these survivals certainly date from an infinitely earlier period than the relatively recent contacts between the pagan, Judaistic, or Christian Berbers and their Islamic conquerors.

When I evoke similarities between the old Arab and old Berber subsoils, I am speaking only about the architecture of the two societies, not about that of the two languages. However, the fact that linguists have related Berber to Semitic obviously reinforces the hypothesis of a very ancient proximity of the peoples who speak these languages.[34] Among possible explanations, it would also be wrong to exclude the hypothesis of a peaceful conquest, whose traces may be followed by archaeologists in aureoles surrounding the Mediterranean Levant: the main conquerors bear the names 'wheat' and 'goat', or if you prefer 'butter' and 'bread'; they certainly did not come alone, and ideas and ways of life undoubtedly figured among their accoutrements.

A few references will indeed be found to an area still wider than that over which the Semitic and Berber tongues are distributed, since it includes regions in which Indo-European languages are spoken. One might be tempted to explain the similarities in question by contact, for the north side of the Mediterranean has often been invaded in the course of the ages by populations from the south, and vice versa. But then why has such and such a custom been borrowed here, and not in another place where the same influence has been exerted. For example, why do certain long-

---

33. It will be seen, particularly in the section of chapter 4 entitled 'Evergreen Foliage and Deciduous Roots', that the structures of a society, though certainly the most fundamental thing about it, are not always the most primordial.

34. Marcel Cohen, *Essai comparatif sur le vocabulaire et la phonétique du chamito-sémitique*, Paris 1947.

converted tribes of Muslim Tuareg continue to disinherit sons in favour of daughters?[35] To veil men and not women? To prefer to marry a boy to the daughter of his maternal uncle rather than to the daughter of his paternal uncle?[36] Why, at the other end of the Muslim world—among the Minangkabau of Sumatra, ardent disciples of Islam[37]—is the hereditary domain transmitted integrally from eldest daughter to eldest daughter, and chattels from maternal uncle to sister's son?

Among the 'fervent' Christians of Sicily, meanwhile, the brother of a noble lady suspected of adultery himself sees to it that she is respectfully strangled before his eyes, in the presence of a chaplain.[38] Murders of this kind, it is true, have not occurred for three or four centuries, but it is only the external form of execution that has changed: for today, Sicilians tend to use a revolver and it is the husband who officiates (since the crime can then be classified as one 'of passion', and suitable arrangements be made with Christian Democratic justice[39]). In country areas of Greece and Lebanon, in similar circumstances, the head of the family still quite often remains faithful to the knife, so young village girls today can be— must be—stabbed most Christianly by their own father, or better still by their elder brother.

In short, there are foreign customs that 'take' like dye, that sink in and become engrained, while others do not, but slide off and are

---

35. All this is changing now, or has already changed, but the change is recent.

36. This is the case with the Tuareg in general, but the Kel Ghela Tuareg prefer to marry young men to the daughters of their maternal aunts, a marriage considered to be incestuous in large parts of the world, even in areas where descent is purely patrilineal.

37. Jeanne Cuisinier, whom we lost in 1964, wrote of the Muslim puritans of Sumatra (the Padri), who from 1804 to 1837 carried on a desperate war first against the traditionalists, then against the Dutch: 'The Padri never protested against the transmission of hereditary goods or their administration by women, any more than they objected to the transmission of names through the mother' (p. 56). She adds: 'The women of Minangkabau are at once more independent and more religious than other Indonesian women' (p. 60). Jeanne Cuisinier, 'Islam et matriarcat à Minangkabau', *Cahiers de Science Économique Appliquée*, July 1963.

38. See chapter 9, 'Women and the Veil'.

39. A minimum penalty for murders 'of honour' has very wisely been set: three years in prison. This helps to avoid the systematic acquittal that was formerly the rule and effectively still is in France. Happily, in France this type of murder has become rare, for it should not be confused with the 'crime of passion'.

wiped out by the launderings of time. So in the Mediterranean basin one reverts to the hypothesis of a very ancient substratum common to the dwellers on its European, Asian, and African shores: in other words, to the Ancient World. Let us not forget that the latter extended well beyond the boundaries of the white race, in Africa and Asia alike.

2
From the Republic of Brothers-in-law to the Republic of Cousins

From the angle of 'elementary structures',[1] the huge area of the world we have just identified can be defined by two features, which coincide geographically: on the one hand, preferential marriage between cousins in the paternal line; on the other, a politics of natality, 'race', and conquest.

A Place Where Incest Is Not Forbidden

I have met groups of noble nomads from the Old World, surviving, albeit moribund almost everywhere:[2] they were still defending the supposed purity of a lineage.[3] Meanwhile, the settled agriculturists I have known in the Maghreb were doubly concerned to avert any risk that foreigners might take, not just their daughters, but their fields too. In an immobile society, this desperate defensive struggle against alien blood inevitably creates its own victims, but they are individual ones. When the society as a whole evolves, bruises multiply and are no longer suffered with the same resignation; a general hardening of systems is then observable. If my hypothesis is correct, Mediterranean women are the great victims of this harden-

---

1. This was the title Claude Lévi-Strauss adopted for his study of the kinship systems of the 'savage world'. Such systems are the exact opposite of the one we shall be analysing. Claude Lévi-Strauss, *The Elementary Structures of Kinship*, London 1968.

2. Except in Mauritania, where 'desert civilization' is still alive and flourishing.

3. Mediterranean and Anglo-Saxon 'racisms' differ: the latter has to do with race (in other words, all lines of ancestry); the former is concerned only with lineage (paternal ancestry).

ing; in and through the women, moreover, all the region's inhabitants suffer grave retardation.

The system of marriage that sociologists call 'endogamous' (in this instance, marriage between first cousins, the children of two brothers) is thus integrated into the social mechanism, with the dangerous consequences we evoked in chapter 1. When we examine the spread of this type of endogamous marriage, we see that it corresponds to a vast and homogeneous region: the entire Old World. We see, too, that this homogeneous region constitutes, as it were, a dark patch upon the kind of structure found everywhere else in the world, for the latter is characterized by an absolute prohibition against marriage between people linked by a legal kinship.[4] In a book that has become an anthropological classic, Claude Lévi-Strauss explains this almost general prohibition of incest by *the necessity of exchange*.[5] Are we to take it, then, that this necessity makes itself felt less strongly in one particular part of the world? Well, that's partly true.

Incest is certainly now prohibited in the Old World, but in a way that even today might still be described as careless.[6] Moreover, we must still agree upon the meaning to be attached to the word 'incest'. If the ethnological sense of 'marriage with a very close relative belonging to your own lineage' is adopted, then it can be argued that throughout the Mediterranean world 'incestuous marriage' is held to be the ideal marriage. We might content ourselves with registering this anomaly without seeking to explain it (thus displaying a virtue much appreciated in ethnography: that of observing and describing everything, while being careful not to interpret it). There is an excuse, however, for devoting this chapter to an ethnography devoid of virtue, and that is the aversion that must be inspired by all conjuring away of questions to which one does not know the answer in advance. Can one really embark on an investigation like this without asking oneself: Why did the Ancient

---

4. Almost everywhere in the Maghreb, 'legal kinship' is constituted by the paternal lineage.

5. See note 1 above.

6. See chapter 3, 'Keeping to Oneself' (on incest in the Mediterranean), and chapter 5, 'Lo, Our Wedding-feast Is Come, O my Brother' (on marriage with a cousin assimilated to a sister: a paternal uncle's daughter).

World (almost, though not quite, in its totality) adopt a preference in the matter of marriage that is the opposite of the one that may be observed among most other populations on earth (most, but not all)?[7] To find the origin of this Mediterranean determination 'not to exchange', to 'keep all the girls in the family for the boys in the family', we shall have to go back a very long way in the history of the human species. At any rate, back beyond the historical level.

A Million Years of Political Argument

There is no question of evoking here all the countless theories as to how the first societies evolved, just a few generally accepted facts concerning their duration. The earliest creature belonging to the human family has been found in south-east Africa, in formations much older than the European ice-ages or the rainy periods that seem to have corresponded to them on the African continent.[8] So he lived in a warm climate and, without either fire or weapons, had to confront the extremely ferocious wild animals who were his contemporaries. There is no shadow of a doubt that even then he lived in groups, and an elementary organization of those groups necessarily constituted his first intelligent activity—long before tool-making, long before speech, long before the mastery of fire (three conquests that were only possible after hundreds of thousands of years of social life and meaningful grunts, adapted to a hierarchy). This explains the extraordinary agility his descendants display and always have displayed, in a domain that still stretches unbroken from the Café du Commerce to the Aranda hordes. For all people on this earth, in fact, have at least a good million years of

---

7. In both cases, it is a question of *majority* positions.
8. On the subject of these creatures, see André Leroi-Gourhan, *Le geste et la parole*, Paris 1964. The author writes on p. 94: 'They walk upright, have arms of normal length, cut standard tools with a few blows struck on the end of a smooth stone. Their diet is partly carnivorous.' This definition certainly corresponds to an ancestor of man and not to a half-monkey, which is why the author has preferred to name him Australanthropos rather than Australopithecus. He adds subsequently (p. 127): '...the presence in the brain of areas of verbal and gesticulatory association is quite conceivable in the case of Australanthropos.'

political argument behind them, a thousand times a thousand years.[9]

Homo, at the dawn of his ascent, was a pretty wretched carnivore: badly equipped for hunting, badly equipped for running away, a prey to larger beasts. This phase of his life extended over the whole immense period of the lower palaeolithic; in other words, it constitutes more than nineteen twentieths of his history. During the last phase of his existence, however, he himself became a great destroyer, who was henceforth to strike fear into the hearts of all other creatures. The turn from one situation to the other—from that of prey to that of hunter—seems to have begun in the middle palaeolithic (Mousterian), hence a little *before* the epoch in which remains of *Homo sapiens* turn up in excavations. For after the middle palaeolithic, *Homo* ceased to be easy prey.

Political Cross-Breeding and the Emergence of Intelligent Man

The first groups of men who, at the dawn of the lower palaeolithic, used fire to warm themselves at night and to protect themselves from wild animals, crossed a threshold that separated them fundamentally from their ancestors. The same can be said of those who, almost a million years later, for the first time fed themselves on cereals they had sown and on meat and milk from animals they had raised.[10] In contrast, there does not seem to have been any such radical difference in way of life between the lower and upper palaeolithic. Nevertheless, it was between the lower and upper palaeolithic—in other words, in the middle palaeolithic—that the mysterious mutation occurred that replaced the low-browed brute of which Neanderthal man is a specimen by the *Homo sapiens* of today. As for the technical inventions that made man the most-feared creature on the planet, these too occurred during the middle palaeolithic; several of them, however, *preceded* the emergence of 'intelligent man'.

---

9. J. Coppens, 'Homo Habilis et les nouvelles découvertes d'Oldoway', *Bulletin de la Société Préhistorique Française*, October 1964.
10. This is a manner of speaking: wild cereals were regularly harvested long before anyone thought of sowing them.

When one considers the anthropological transformations that still occur today in a human group whose way of life is altered,[11] it is easy to be convinced that something important was changed in the habits of palaeolithic men just before the upper palaeolithic, a change that explains the appearance of *Homo sapiens*. But what precisely?

Fire, of course, must certainly have been used for thousands of years as a defence against wild beasts and cold before it was ever used to cook most foodstuffs: eating habits do not change easily even today, and ingenuity is required to cook certain vegetables without a pot.[12] So it is possible that the habit of cooking (and thus rendering assimilable) a significant portion of man's food came later than one might be tempted to imagine, and this undoubtedly influenced man's physical, mental, and social evolution.

All the same, recent prehistoric discoveries have signally narrowed the gap separating us from the middle palaeolithic, Mousterian industry, and Neanderthal man,[13] thereby increasing the distance between the latter and the first humans who used fire. That gives food for thought.

In this new perspective, it is perhaps not absurd to imagine a different kind of change, social and not technological: an 'institution' responding to the growing shortage of game. This shortage probably reached its apogee *soon* after the first technological inventions of the middle palaeolithic (traps, throwing weapons, the use

---

11. According to Kluckhohn, 'The researches of Boas, Shapiro, and others have cast doubt on the fixity of these characteristics [shape of head, height]. German and Russian children who suffered from the famines following the First World War differed markedly from their parents both in stature and in head-form. Over longer time-spans the changes are still more startling. For example, one group of "Nordics" appears to have become twelve points more round-headed between 1200 BC and AD 1935.' Clyde Kluckhohn, *Mirror for Man*, London 1950, p. 112.

12. The prairie Indians boiled water in leather vats by throwing in scorching stones; in the Pyrenees, cheese is still sometimes manufactured by throwing hot stones into the milk. People who do not practise these somewhat complicated cooking methods may roast chestnuts and even bake bread in the ashes (I have done this in the Ahaggar, and in the Aïr: it is excellent).

13. In Europe, Neanderthal man disappeared about thirty-five thousand years ago, and his presence has been attested over a period lasting more than one hundred and fifteen thousand years. When prehistorians still thought that man's existence went back only three hundred thousand years, *Homo neanderthalensis* was a very distant ancestor. He has, however, drawn far closer to us since the adventure of our species has been reckoned at two million years.

of beaters in hunting). For it was necessarily compensated for thereafter, by something we can only call 'covenants', or sets of rules, whereas immediately after the technological inventions dearth took humanity by surprise. The situation throughout the middle and upper palaeolithic was, in fact, exactly the opposite of our own: progress created scarcity, human intelligence caused famine, but these famines were necessarily preceded by conflicts among the hunters. In the upper palaeolithic, however, no trace of these struggles can be found. May these scarcities, from the middle palaeolithic onwards, perhaps have obliged men to invent—this time not in the sphere of technology, but in the sphere of politics?

What makes this hypothesis plausible (or at least not unlikely) is the ethnographical experience: for this does indeed show us a literally unrestrained social inventiveness among all 'savages', combined everywhere with a fairly poor and slow technological inventiveness. This alone is one good reason for supposing that politics is associated with our evolution right from its first beginnings. A neighbouring science—prehistory—provides us with another argument, drawn from long musings before the glass cases in which the earliest human tools are ranged. Our ancestors' almost infinite capacity for imitation is astonishing when one sees them copying the same tool for tens of thousands of years. It is hard not to assume a parallel conservatism with respect to institutions. Yet suddenly, forty thousand years ago (a long time in comparison with the five thousand years of historical time, but very little in terms of the two million years of our evolution), human progress undergoes an acceleration that no discernible reason can account for. Almost immediately afterwards, a species of man appears who is already our contemporary; and almost at once, the creation of real works of art begins to bear witness to his genius.

Whatever the nature of the change that preceded the appearance of present-day humanity, it was important and decisive. Yet there is no sign of it in excavations of the period in question, which provide indications only of a significant improvement over a previous way of life: hitherto badly equipped hunters now invent weapons and organize themselves, which allows them to become much more of a threat to their quarry. But they continue to be hunters, fishermen, and collectors of acorns, chestnuts or wild millet. And yet, they undergo a radical change of physical and intellectual type. In the region that concerns us (North Africa, Europe, the Levant), no remains of *Homo sapiens* are found in formations older than forty millennia; but as soon as they appear, the signs of an intelligent human activity multiply. From then on, every technological advance will bring an additional chance of survival for our species, and hence a numerical increase.[14] But until the neolithic, nature will penalize this increase just as it does that of rabbits or squirrels: by shortage of food, thus leading to death or enforced emigration.

However, it emerges that the men of the upper palaeolithic did not emigrate much, unlike the peoples of the following (neolithic) period, and André Leroi-Gourhan has written (regarding the sea shells found in deposits from this epoch): 'In short, in most cases supplies seem to have come from within a radius of one hundred to two hundred kilometres, which fits in well with available information on the existence of relatively stable regional groups within the great complex constituted by the palaeolithic West.'[15] He further notes (in connection with rock paintings): 'Study of these works, where they have been found in sufficient density, shows that the regional units were solid and stable for long centuries. Between the Solutrean and the recent Magdalenian, Asturias, Cantabrians, Central Pyrenees, regions of Quercy and the Dordogne—all display a really striking individuality of style; the Rhône valley too seems to have constituted a continuous geographical entity. It would be a serious error to conceive of prehistoric peoples as careering turbulently around the immense spaces between the Atlantic and the Urals: the palaeolithic world does not seem to have been very different from the historical world.'[16]

---

14. V. Gordon Childe, *Man Makes Himself*, London 1934, p. 66: 'The deep Upper Palaeolithic deposits in the caves, the masses of tools that can be collected, suggest an increased population. The number of Upper Palaeolithic skeletons found in France alone exceeds that of all earlier skeletons put together. Yet the period over which they must be distributed is not one-twentieth of that to which the latter belong. Nevertheless, the number of Upper Palaeolithic skeletons is not one-hundredth of that attributed to the neolithic period in France, which did not last a fifth of the time assigned to the Aurignacian and Magdalenian phases.'

15. André Leroi-Gourhan, *Les religions de la préhistoire*, Paris 1964, p. 72.

16. Ibid., p. 84.

Even if food shortages caused by growing scarcity of game arose only in the upper palaeolithic, survival still remained 'the problem' confronting men for *a hundred, two hundred, three hundred centuries*—six times longer than the entire span of history. And if one accepts that the shortages may have begun back in the middle palaeolithic, then this vast period of time must be reckoned at more than forty millennia, a time during which human intelligence was continuously faced with one overriding necessity: to maintain a balance between man's numbers and the spaces from which he drew his food.

At all events, the length of time was quite sufficient for the old clan headsmen's sociological reflection to have explored every dimension countless times. In practice, this reflection must ultimately have leaned towards, and then settled upon (by way of a thousand absurd fancies, something of which has come down to us), the only possible, *rational* solution: to protect the game and, in the social sphere, to create and maintain a status quo, namely respect for one's neighbour's frontiers and grazing lands.[17] This would explain, in particular, the relative stability of this period's settlements. But it would also explain the prevalence of that complicated institution known as exogamy, which is still practised on all continents by peoples who live mainly by hunting and gathering. It would also explain why the first works of art were inspired by what the first prehistorians called the fertility cult: systematic protection of female animals and, by a logical extension, attention to human natality (the two appear from the Aurignacian epoch onwards).

We know that palaeolithic man depended upon resources whose yield he could not increase without running the risk of destroying irreparably the fauna and flora that fed him. Judging by the diggings inventorized to date, it seems that he did not have recourse to

---

17. Kluckhohn, p. 58: 'It is not certain that warfare existed during the earlier part of the New Stone Age in Europe and the Orient. Settlements lack structures that would have defended them against attack. Weapons seem to be limited to those needed in hunting animals.... Organized, offensive warfare was unknown in aboriginal Australia. Certain areas of the New World seem to have been completely free from war in the pre-European period.' Indeed, the absence of war does characterize the upper palaeolithic, but not the neolithic (see p. 50).

war. No sign of cannibalism is to be discerned among the human remains that have come down to us. We find the population growing abruptly after the neolithic discoveries, but it seems to be stable during the entire palaeolithic: people do not emigrate, hardly increase in numbers, do not kill each other. Why? How? What can safely be asserted, at all events, is that some explanation is needed.

On the other hand, the strange social invention of exogamy—complicated, difficult to operate, extremely frustrating for those who practise it,[18] and whose utility is not immediately obvious,[19] is today so widely diffused in the human species that there is no continent where traces of it are not to be found, in a quite inconceivable range of extravagant combinations. When this distribution is considered, it becomes necessary either to admit some 'requirement' of human society (but how is one then to explain the existence of a huge, homogeneous zone—the entire Ancient World[20]—where this law characteristic of human society in general fails to apply), or to seek an explanation that takes account of the two contrasted solutions. If the relationship between the Mediterranean neolithic and endogamy (which seems fairly probable to me) is accepted, then the origins of exogamy must be pushed back to an immeasurably more ancient past, certainly a palaeolithic one. At that level, one is then obliged to seek no longer an invariable law (since it has varied[21]), but an adventitious phenomenon, at once very primitive, very general, and very imperative.

Scarcity, caused by an improvement in hunting techniques, corresponds quite well to those conditions. Effectively, only four consequences were possible: emigration, inter-tribal war, disappearance through famine, or the quest for a status quo. Now, we have seen that the men of the upper palaeolithic did not emigrate much; they do not seem to have practised war or cannibalism; they undoubtedly dominated their geographical environment; their

18. See pp. 57–8 below.
19. In *Elementary Structures*, Lévi-Strauss effectively disposes of those theories that explain the incest prohibition in terms of morality, hygiene, etc.
20. Chapter 3 is devoted to the endogamy that characterized the Ancient World, and chapter 5 to present-day endogamy.
21. It will be seen, in chapters 3 and 5, *how* it varied within a very extensive area centred on the Mediterranean.

numbers very gradually increased. In other words, these observations, taken together, exclude both the hypothesis of a squandering of natural resources (which would then have caused a local disappearance of our species) and that of a *natural* birth-rate.

The men of the upper palaeolithic (Aurignacians, Magdalenians) possessed a brain no different from that of present day man—this is what the skulls that have been found suggest. Did they also have an intelligence comparable to our own? It is quite true that the harnessing of intelligence is a social fact, which can therefore be modified in the course of time; but as we well know, this harnessing is not sufficient, but requires a basis: the brain. The latter is far more slowly modified, and has not been modified since the appearance of *Homo sapiens*, despite the enormous changes that have taken place. Are we then to assume that the change that interfered with human habits at the end of the middle palaeolithic was more important than all the changes our species has experienced during the past hundred centuries?

The Palaeo-Political Age

In a society that lives by hunting and gathering, any group that survives will first of all have preserved the species that provide it with food, and to this end will have concentrated its attention upon the survival of the females. Second, it will have had to keep a close watch on itself, to avoid either diminishing in number or growing (which means it will have had to keep a strict eye on its birth-rate; neither too may, nor too few children). Finally, it will have had to protect its living-space against incursions by its neighbours. Now, exogamy constitutes an immediate means to establish a network of treaties; but, once installed, it can also play a part in the transformation of "natural" into "social" birth-rates.[22] It can also help old clan headsmen to appropriate young maidens preferentially.

---

22. We may note, in connection with this, that the 'natural birth-rate' (one child per year for all women aged between fifteen and forty-five) is not found in any society, savage or otherwise. At most, it could be encountered some years ago among Canadian Catholics.

It is by no means rash to believe that by the end of the upper palaeolithic *Homo* had long 'observed' exogamy in all its aspects, that he had played around with it, and that in all probability he was already aware of—and could evaluate—the brake it effectively places on the birth-rate. It is far more rash to imagine this custom, not at the end of the upper palaeolithic—a period highly advanced in art and technology, and undoubtedly also in institutions—but immediately following the first great inventions that mark the middle palaeolithic, which definitively reverse man's position relative to his environment: henceforward, he will be less and less endangered, more and more dangerous.

We may imagine that the first conventions regulated conflicts between groups whose common origin was recent; we may imagine that these conventions become customs; we may imagine that, when different human groups later found themselves in frontier contact, the one that used the system of exchanging women to maintain peace managed to get the idea across to the newcomers. Then centuries and millennia went by. Is it possible to attribute the invention of exogamy to Neanderthal man, the 'low-browed brute'? What we know of his tools does not make this improbable; nor is it improbable to suppose that each group of hunters was already seeking to reserve hunting grounds for itself. Frontiers and boundaries imply conventions and systems of alliance, of which the simplest and most 'primitive' is, indeed, exchange of women.

If this set of hypotheses is accepted, two astonishing phenomena of human history can perhaps be explained: first, the appearance of modern man, intelligent man, *Homo sapiens*; second, the no less surprising and simultaneous disappearance of all the other representatives of the genus *Homo*. In this view, *Homo sapiens* was born of systematic political cross-breeding among previously existing human stocks, and it was *into him* that they all disappeared. In short, 'intelligent man' was manufactured, an invention (undoubtedly the greatest of all) that must be attributed to Neanderthal man, the 'low-browed brute' of our childhood textbooks. In order to ensure the safety of his hunting areas, he must have managed, from the Mousterian age onwards, to subject himself to the rough discipline of exogamy, thus setting in train a process of systematic crossing that stretched over the thirty thousand years of the upper palaeolithic.

Let us remember that, until the neolithic, technological progress necessarily and continually encountered one stumbling-block: scarcity, an automatic result of the improvements introduced into hunting and gathering practices. Logically, this stumbling-block should have directed the best minds of the entire period towards political invention and magical inquiry. Well, the fact is that in civilizations comparable to theirs today (ones living mainly by hunting and gathering), the wealth of political inventiveness leaves all the specialists who study them flabbergasted.[23]

One fine day, one fine century, everything changes radically: *Homo* has invented the cultivation of cereals (in other words, agriculture); domestication of the goat, sheep, and cow (in other words, stock-rearing);[24] and the town (in other words, civilization). All this at more or less the same time (to within five or six centuries), and in more or less the same place. Moreover, the inventors took to polishing stones instead of cutting them, which facilitated the working of wood and hence navigation and haulage; and this practice, which gave its name (neolithic) to their culture as a whole, spread with it. For, since the beginning of time, civilizations have been adopted or rejected en bloc.

These neolithic inventions were preceded or followed by many others—weaving, pottery, navigation by dugout or raft, cartage by sledge or dog-sleigh—whose net result was to change the face of planet earth quite rapidly, by accelerating human evolution. To measure their importance, it is enough to note that almost two million years went by between the appearance of the first hominids and the beginnings of the neolithic revolution,[25] but only about eight thousand years—ten thousand at most—between the latter

---

23. After the discoveries of the neolithic, it was technological invention that became the priority. For anyone who came (as I did) by way of ethnology to a study of the ancient rural societies of the Old World, it is striking to compare the poverty of invention of these societies in the domain of institutions and structures with the wealth evident in exogamous societies.

24. The dog was domesticated at the end of the palaeolithic or at the beginning of the mesolithic, a very long time before the goat and sheep, which came a little before the cow. 'The likeliest candidate for the title of grandfather of the goats is the so-called bezoar-goat of Turkestan and Afghanistan. The winner of the sheep contest seems to be the argal of the Elburz Mountains in northern Iran.... Sheep and goat coincide geographically with wheat.' Carleton C. Coon, *The History of Man*, London 1955, p. 130.

25. See note 13 above.

and ourselves. From this juncture on, time would be reckoned in centuries instead of millennia. Yet we must not forget that such a leap forward could never have occurred if the palaeolithic hunts-men had not long possessed a brain and manual dexterity equal to our own, which implies mastery of a great many ideas. Perhaps it would be appropriate to call the upper palaeolithic 'the palaeo-political age', the better to distinguish it from the following period, which could be termed the 'palaeo-technological'.[26]

In the course of the neolithic, the innumerable regulations in-vented by the sleepless geniuses of the caves were to be abrogated. Restraint would no longer be necessary: one would be able to hunt and ravage at will, for one's herds and fields would safeguard the future. One would also be able to keep one's own women, take one's neighbour's, and have as many children as might result, for the more numerous one was, the stronger one would be in defend-ing and augmenting a nascent capitalization.

The Infant 'Civilization' Dandled on Bony Knees

The birth of the world's first towns was roughly contemporary, and roughly coextensive, with humanity's most decisive discoveries: cereal cultivation and animal domestication. These inventions were essentially rural, to be sure, but no more rural than the first cities. Perhaps archaelogy will one day allow us to resolve definitively the problem of priority among these three great creations—town, field, herd—which emerged right back in prehistory. However that may be, I am tempted in the meantime to postulate that the town was the first of the three to arrive, for it seems to me to have been the greatest inventive factor in our entire evolution.

I know that the sacred texts of Sociology declare the opposite, with vigorously logical arguments.[27] It is very true, moreover, that *town* means *specialization*, or if you prefer *craftsmen*, and hence *food surplus*; and it is logical to think that this 'surplus' was possi-ble only after the great neolithic inventions of agriculture and stock-rearing. But on the other hand, ethnologists know that

---

26. See note 23 above.
27. Engels, for example, in *Origin of the Family, Private Property and the State.*

isolated men do not invent, or hardly invent;[28] and prehistorians are accustomed to reckoning the time it takes a very minor technological advance to spread in thousands of years. Yet all of a sudden progress is measured no longer in thousands of years but in centuries or even quarter-centuries; and it abruptly begins to respond to all the great human needs at once.

Between sociological and ethnological improbability, only archaeology will be able to adjudicate.[29] While we await its verdict, there is nothing to stop us imagining, near a fish-filled lake or river, one spot where fishing is particularly rewarding; and not far from there, flooded lands that allow an abundant and regular harvesting of wild cereals. A bitter conflict breaks out between two large groups, and its more efficient social organization gives one of them victory. It then fortifies the coveted position, establishes a market—and a town is born. From that moment on, true progress is under way, every invention being immediately disseminated, imitated, perfected. So the two great scourges of humanity, tyranny and war, have apparently dandled the little nascent civilization on their bony knees.

For the moment, let us confine ourselves to asserting that the sociological hypothesis is no more certain than this alternative, but that in one way or another the events took place on the same little portion of our planet and—give or take a very few centuries—at the same instant. Very little time, in any case, if we consider that the 'fashion' of the lower palaeolithic's heavy bi-facial flints lasted for hundreds of thousands of years almost without variation, a span almost ten times as long as the immense period we are assuming here for exogamy. Very soon, then, men stopped fearing shortages due to the improvement of hunting techniques (those advances which rebounded so quickly on their inventors, by accelerating both the rate at which game was exterminated and the rate at which hunters proliferated). But more and more they must have

---

28. Even more than by the simple aggregation of brains, progress is advanced by contact between intelligences, which ignites genius: the small organized cities of ancient Greece were more productive than our shanty towns.

29. Archaeological discoveries postdating the first edition of this study confirm its hypothesis.

come to fear the attacks of less favoured groups upon those vulnerable and attractive targets: barns and herds.

In direct contrast to what seems to be the case during the previous period, during the neolithic archaeology allows us to discern numerous changes, on the vast spaces between the Nile and the Ganges. As Gordon Childe has written: 'Radical and sometimes catastrophic changes in pottery and domestic architecture, in art and burial rites, are in reality discernible in the settlement mounds of Iran, Mesopotamia, and Syria, and in the cemeteries of Egypt. Such changes are generally held to indicate displacements of population, the conquest or invasion by and infiltration of new peoples.'[30] Clyde Kluckhohn, on the other hand, reports that the first neolithic villages show no sign of fortifications.[31] Yet in 1961 I had a chance to view the diggings, still in progress, on the site of the oldest town identified so far (Jericho). They have uncovered a 'village' extending over more than three hectares, which was protected by a ditch nine metres wide and three metres deep, hollowed out of the rock.[32] The inhabitants contemporary with the oldest level raised sheep and goats, but not cattle; they did not polish their stone axes, were ignorant of pottery, and lived nine thousand years ago (date provided by Carbon 14).[33] The round stone tower and the enormous wall that buttressed it seemed to me very like a rampart. And rampart means town—and war. Did war follow progress? Or did progress follow war? Whichever theory is adopted to explain the change, change there was, and one that called the entire human experience into question again.

Were the Wives of Aurignacian Hunters Less Robust Than the Norman Women of Quebec?

At the dawn of the neolithic, the world was very sparsely inhabited. As Jean Fourastié has written: 'A figure of ten million people has been suggested for the entire planet at the start of the

---

30. Childe, *Man Makes Himself*, p. 145.
31. Quoted in note 17 above.
32. K. Kenyon, 'Communication', *Revue Biblique*, vol. 64, 1956, p. 225.
33. Average figure: 8,225 years, for the second phase. It has not been possible to date the first phase.

fourth millennium BC: this is roughly the present-day population of the Tokyo municipality. ... The hundred-million mark was reached, we think, at the time of Christ; so at that moment (in other words, very recently in the history of our species) the French and Italians of today would still have peopled the five continents on their own. The thousand-million mark was reached around 1830. In 1962, we were 3,135,000,000. Current trends suggest that six thousand million will be attained by the year 2000. A fairly unlikely drop in the fertility rate would be needed for the twelve-thousand-million mark not to be achieved in 2050 or 2060.'[34] If, instead of studying the growth of the human species on a global scale, we examine it within the confines of French territory—in prehistoric terms, one of the best known areas in the world—we find that between the time when the population was culturally palaeolithic and the time when it had become neolithic, it multiplied tenfold.[35] No more explosive rate of human increase occurs until the twentieth century. The difference between the two periods is that at the beginning of the neolithic the earth was almost empty, whereas today it is almost full.

All the same, let us pause a moment to marvel. A few hundred French peasants leave Normandy in the seventeenth century; two hundred years later, they have ten million descendants.[36] Was Canada in the eighteenth century more salubrious than the valley of

---

34. Jean Fourastié, *Les 40,000 heures*, Paris 1964, p. 158.

35. Louis-René Nougier, 'Les genres de vie de l'homme préhistorique', *La Nature*, March 1953, p. 83: 'By qualitative methods, it is possible to arrive at a plausible estimate of the population of Gaul in the third millennium before our era. The rural distribution of rich, easily worked land suggests a density of the order of ten or twenty inhabitants per square kilometre. But the whole territory was not so densely populated. In particular, the Armorican massif, the Massif Central and the Alps largely escaped neolithic settlement. Regions like Burgundy, Normandy, and the agricultural lands of the Oise, on the other hand, seem to have been more heavily populated. If one takes all these different factors into account, according to the all-too-rare accurate maps established, the neolithic population of Gaul may have reached five million inhabitants at the end of the third millennium. Estimates for the fourth, however, cannot go above half a million.... We may reflect that four millennia were to be required, from the end of the third millennium BC to our twentieth century, for the same territory once again to increase its population tenfold.'

36. French emigration to Canada halted under Louis XV, and started up again only very recently. (To the numbers in Canada, one must add the numerous francophones who emigrated from Canada to the United States.) The present population

the Dordogne fifteen thousand years ago? Were the contemporaries of Henri IV more healthy or more fertile than Cro-Magnon women? But if not, how are we to explain the slow demographic growth so unmistakable among our palaeolithic ancestors, and which we find among all hunting peoples? 'That's the way it is', reply the statisticians. 'We know that population grows with food resources.' But how are we to explain the fact that this miraculous, mysterious law of growth has stopped functioning in three quarters of the world, even in our own epoch?

What if a different assumption were made? Suppose we had *social* habits of demographic balance—slowly, arduously, and painfully acquired and maintained over the four hundred intelligent centuries that preceded the neolithic. Then, seven or eight thousand years ago, they gave way, like a spring being released, as a result of inventions that made it possible to increase and stock food. The peoples affected were henceforward to multiply enormously—even more than they wished to—but this numerical development was itself to be a crucial factor of conquest, and likewise of invention.

Then, one fine day, thanks to the compass and to Christopher Columbus, they met 'savages'—in other words, peoples having a 'status quo' tradition[37]—and, of course, the encounter was fatal to the latter, who from now on would be out of the running. In the twentieth century, it was to be within the great swathe of 'natalist' populations that a tragic split would occur: for one part of the peoples of the Ancient World, of the first civilized inhabitants of the planet, of the first beneficiaries of the neolithic demographic explosion (the senior branch), is now heading for the famine its populating tradition creates; while another part of the same population (the Europo-American, cadet branch), thanks to

---

of Canada is 19 million, of whom almost half are of French origin. The Canadian demographic explosion predates the great medical discoveries.

37. I prefer this expression to such descriptions as 'palaeolithic tradition' or 'living mainly by hunting, fishing, and gathering' or 'exogamous', for the peoples in question have (more or less belatedly and sporadically) known neolithic techniques, and have often practised a little agriculture and stock-rearing, though not enough to uproot a tradition of demographic prudence, which seems to me to characterize them.

another series of inventions,[38] has returned to the demographic prudence of the cave men.

The Hundred Square Kilometres of a Palaeolithic Family

The first palaeolithic men were not entirely men, and the last were probably politicians beset by problems. To find the image of *Homo* setting off to conquer the world — Adam — one should perhaps look in the early years of the neolithic. The beautiful but still wild land of the Mediterranean shores, a wonderful climate, a virgin soil where goats, peasants and pharaohs had not yet decimated the forests and where one needed to sow only the best alluvial earth. It is easy to imagine the prodigious changes agriculture and stock-rearing brought to men's lives there, and the impetus they gave to men's hopes. To suggest a scale of comparison, let us recall the figure Vidal de La Blache was so fond of quoting in connection with the Cambodian rice-fields: a hectare there is enough to support a family. More space is needed for corn-eaters in a dry zone, and much more again for pastors. But how are we to calculate the area required to support a household of Magdalenian hunters? As a rough guide, let us look at the estimates made for the 'savage continents', before men arrived from the Old World. One inhabitant per square kilometer in the most densely populated region, that is to say the north-west coast of America—but its population was so dense only because it fed off a 'game' impossible to decimate without the help of an industrial technology: salmon. For the Pacific coast of America as a whole, eighteen inhabitants per hundred square kilometers—once again, fishermen. With prairie hunters, the population density goes down by half: only eight per hundred square kilometres. On another continent (Australia), two inhabitants per thousand square kilometres.[39]

With the neolithic, the vital equation was reversed, since henceforth resources would increase *pari passu* with population, and for thousands of years almost never would there be too many arms to

---

38. The large-scale industry of the nineteenth century.
39. V. Gordon Childe, *What Happened in History*, Harmondsworth 1978, p. 52.

work the fields, make ploughs, protect grain reserves, or defend livestock (our peasants still speak of someone going to 'guard' cattle). It seems likely that this change—so radical and localized—had repercussions on the way the men of those days 'theorized' their societies. But I would like to stress that this shift cannot be attributed to one invention rather than to another, but only to the shock represented by the combination of all those inventions in a determinate area and at a determinate period, and above all by its almost immediate consequence: *a sharp variation in man's relationship with the space that fed him.*[40]

For it is a fact that the societies arranged in concentric circles around the privileged region in which *Homo* first put a herd out to pasture and sowed a field are expansionist (strictly forbidding birth-control[41]); endogamous to the very brink of incest (and sometimes beyond it);[42] 'racist'; and warlike. And it is also a fact that these societies engendered our civilization. By contrast, scattered over all the remaining portions of continents, so-called primitive cultures have maintained themselves in which men live by hunting, gathering, or rudimentary agriculture—at all events, within a static economy. These, according to my hypothesis, have continued unbroken the 'status quo' tradition I believe was that of *Homo sapiens* up to the neolithic revolution. For their way of life has obliged them to study and observe for themselves how to maintain a balance. And what balance but, in practice, family planning and an embryonic United Nations?

---

40. As early as 1938, while observing the changes that had occurred in less than a generation among the transhumant pastors of the southern Aurès, I had come to the conclusion that the prime cause of social mutation was a variation in population density. I gave a lecture at the CHEAM on this subject, between my second and third field trips (1938).

41. 'Westermarck tells us that foeticide and infanticide are common practices among nomadic peoples. Children of tender age are elements of weakness. Perhaps our rule—and another closely related one, also drawn from the so-called laws of Romulus, forbidding the exposure of infants—are reactions by an agricultural people against earlier practices.' Pierre Noailles, 'Les tabous du mariage dans le droit primitif des Romains', *Annales Sociologiques*, Series C, section 2, p. 11 (referring to Westermarck, *L'origine et le développement des idées morales*, Paris 1928, p. 420).

42. See above, in this chapter.

Let us call the former, our own societies, 'natalist': they correspond to the impact of the first neolithic civilization.[43] For the latter, let us keep the name 'savage'. Among 'savage' techniques for birth-control and international peace,[44] we may then evoke the incest prohibition and exchange of women[45]—but probably also marriage, monogamy,[46] and even virtue, institutions that have thus outlived the causes that gave rise to them. One must, however, add to these some less admired methods for regulating births: notably infanticide,[47] and perhaps human sacrifice. As for cannibalism, it was an obvious solution; if we find no trace of it we should be astonished and speak quite intrepidly of spiritual motives. Conversely, neolithic sociology[48] (our own) can claim credit for prohibiting exchange, returning to incest, polygamy, war, 'racism', slavery, and a veritable obsession with female

43. This does not, of course, mean that there are no neolithic techniques among 'savages', but merely that the impact of the early neolithic was concentrated upon the Ancient World.
44. In a society influenced by the Ancient World, but whose mode of production has remained palaeolithic (the Tuareg), one finds a 'primitive' birth-rate, by which I mean one that is the opposite of 'natural' (see pp. 117–8).
45. Lévi-Strauss has shown in *Elementary Structures* that these two customs go together.
46. It was likewise cause for astonishment among the first anthropologists when they observed the frequency of monogamy among their 'savages'. Schmidt senior (Marcel Mauss's great adversary) deduced a moral sociology from this. Furthermore, in the event of war, the exchange of women or men was regularly practised until a short time ago among very archaic peoples, despite a declared 'racist' stance. I have noted several early instances of the exchange of men between Taitoq and Kel Ghela (matrilineal descent). Barth records exchanges of women between the white Kel Owey (whom he calls the pale conquerors) and the indigenous blacks of the Altgober region: they apparently even concluded a treaty obliging the chief of the Kel Owey only to marry a black woman (this region, I believe, has patrilineal descent). Duveyrier, for his part, tells us that when one points out to noble Tuareg that they are very dark-skinned, they invoke the 'policy' which, in the event of a defeat or victory, obliges them to hand over or receive a yearly contingent of young virgins. Duveyrier, *Les Touaregs du Nord*, Paris 1864.
47. 'While the child is being delivered, the father waits within earshot until its sex is determined, when the midwives call it out to him. To this information he answers laconically, "Wash it" or "Do not wash it". If the command is "Wash it", the child is to be brought up. In a few cases, when the child is a girl and there are already several girl-children in the family, the child will not be saved.' Mead, *Sex and Temperament*, p. 32.
48. We are concerned here not with the neolithic on a world scale, but with the first neolithic, localized in the Mediterranean Levant.

virginity[49]—without forgetting the 'natalist' policy that can be found in most societies of the Ancient World and there alone. It is possible (but not certain) that to these may be added a notable predilection for vendettas, patrilineal descent, and privileges for the eldest son.

Human Space, the Structures of Kinship, and Two Types of Natality

In short, since he emerged from the animal condition, man has twice known an earth that was too big for him, twice one that was too small: too big during the entire lower palaeolithic (almost two thousand millennia); too small at the time of the great Magdalenian, Aurignacian, and even Mousterian hunters (twenty, thirty, or forty thousand years); then once again too big when civilization was born with the neolithic nine thousand years ago. Now, in this second half of the twentieth century, it is for the second time too small, thanks to the discoveries of Pasteur, Fleming, and a few others. And this, very obviously, is the most significant fact of our age.

These hypotheses fit in with the relative continuity of the upper palaeolithic civilizations, the turbulence of the following period, and the existence of two world zones, each characterized by a particular type of structure. They also make it possible to explain the distribution of the 'savage structure' over a territory so vast and discontinuous that those who have studied it have tended to apply evolutionist theories to it, whereas in the (compact) zone of the great civilizations scholars have tended to invoke diffusionist theories to explain facts of the same kind. It likewise explains why, against all logic, it should be the 'savage zone' that subjected itself to the rough discipline and complexities of exchange of women and commodities; while in the Ancient World, where humanity

---

49. I imagine it is with the Iberian tradition rather than the Indian subculture that one should connect the story (commonplace in the Brazilian north-east) of the practising Catholic who remarried without taking the trouble to divorce, because in all good faith he considered his first marriage null and void. The reason: his first wife had not been a virgin. I was told the poor man was really crestfallen and surprised when he discovered that he was a bigamist.

developed furthest the features that characterize it—I mean, that distinguish it from other living species—an effort was made to avoid this essential 'human' feature wherever possible.

We find ourselves, in short, in the presence of two universes, which differ in age but have, on occasion, coincided in time. Each is ruled by physical laws of its own. The former, static social universe is characterized by great duration over a vast expanse. It is the one the palaeolithic hunters constructed during the thirty millennia of the upper palaeolithic; the one, too, that survived in the 'new worlds', where science discovered it in the nineteenth century and at once (not without good reasons) presumed to see it as a stage in a past common to our entire species. The second social universe is an 'expanding universe', more localized than the former, since it corresponds to an 'event', or rather to a series of converging events: those which Gordon Childe very rightly called the 'neolithic revolution'. That means they can be dated, at least approximately, and their centre of dispersal can also be situated geographically: it corresponds to that of the Ancient World. On the one hand, status quo policies worked out in the most highly developed of the 'savage' cultures—in other words, among intelligent people living only by hunting and gathering. On the other, natalist policies linked with a type of economy in which production grows indefinitely: our own, to date.

The Neolithic 'Situation' Reproduces Certain Aspects of Man's Earliest State

If a link is conceded between the structural evolution of societies and man's relationship with the space that feeds him, it can then be perceived that the neolithic 'situation' reproduced certain aspects of an infinitely older one: that of the lower palaeolithic, shrouded in the great shadow of our ignorance. We may, however, imagine that the space was then too great around hordes constantly threatened with extinction. Now, it is also known that these conditions of life and the feelings they engendered (the only authentically primitive ones of the human past) lasted for hundreds of millennia, a span so immense that it is certainly deep in that infinite night that the roots of what we call 'human nature' must be sought.

Actually, one has the clear impression that many neolithic features are more 'natural', more 'primitive', and less 'frustrating' to what seem to be our most instinctive requirements—in short, less 'social'—than those of so-called savage civilizations. At all events, examples of the frustrating and complicated character of the 'savage civilizations' abound in ethnographic literature, and the annoyance this causes the men who impose it upon themselves has been noted. Meyer Fortes, for example, has described the 'resentment constantly expressed by Ashanti of both sexes and all stations in life against the restraints and frustrations which they attribute to the observance of the rule of matrilineal descent'.[50] On the other side of the Atlantic, among the Indians, Claude Lévi-Strauss has signalled the same reactions. We shall also see in chapter 7 ('Conflict with God') that the good grace with which the Tuareg adopted certain Islamic prescriptions derives from their antipathy towards their previous institutions.

In this view of economic prehistory, there is no longer any reason to be surprised at finding that the structures of each of these universes are, in both cases, so rich in internal contradictions. For the proliferation of humanity (which, for the Ancient World, resulted from the neolithic discoveries) simply imposed upon it the communication it rejected—and communication means progress; while the other social hemisphere, the 'savage', which conceived and institutionalized exchange, has remained the world of great isolation. One could also explain the survivals, in each of the two systems, of customs and aspirations (always the most archaic) belonging to the opposite system. For in the (endogamous) Ancient World, one meets elements of social structures that can be understood only in an exogamous system.[51] In the Maghreb, I have

---

50. Meyer Fortes, 'Kinship and Marriage Among the Ashanti', in the collective work edited by A.R. Radcliffe-Brown and D. Forde, *African Systems of Kinship and Marriage*, Oxford 1950, p. 262.

51. In relation to exogamy, Marcel Mauss was fond of quoting the examples mentioned by Hubert and Czarnowski among the Celts: 'In the history of Munster two royal houses appear, Clanna Deirgthene and Clanna Dairenne, which hold the power generation about, *intermarry, and put their children out to board with each other.*' (The institution that consists in having sons brought up by foster-parents—known by the Anglo-Norman term 'fosterage'—long survived in Celtic areas, and in Ireland was called *altram.*) Henri Hubert, *The Greatness and Decline*

searched for them carefully and can cite several:[52] they seem to me to be ancient and 'internal to the society', as ancient and integral as the facts of endogamy; they are simply very rare and localized. It is true that once accepted, any evolutionist theory can engender the image of a 'civilized' society succeeding a 'savage' one, and preserving some of its traits. The reverse would be more surprising. Yet the reliable, sensitive observer of the 'Elementary Structures' chose to end his book by quoting an Andaman myth concerning the future life: when 'all will remain in the prime of life, sickness and death will be unknown, and there will be no more marrying or giving in marriage.' And the French author speaks to us of the 'joys, eternally denied to social man, of a world in which one might keep to oneself'.[53] 'Keeping to oneself': this could be the title of the present study, for it is precisely the formula that fits the relentless will whose tracks we are now going to follow on almost every page. And it is that relentless will—where it came up against impossibilities—which, in my view, debased the female condition throughout the Mediterranean basin.

As for the hypotheses we have just examined, before relegating them to the vast herbarium of outdated theories, let us at least retain a number of elements that seem to me fairly certain or at least plausible, all concerning endogamy. First of all, its diffusion: it is already widespread at the point when history begins, and an origin long predating this is suggested; yet this origin, albeit so ancient

of the Celts, London 1934, p. 201. However, Hubert also (p. 203) quotes Strabo, and Strabo (repeating Pytheas) says of the Irish that they used to boast of respecting neither mother nor sister (see chapter 3, 'Keeping to Oneself'). For Czarnowski, see Stefan Czarnowski, *Le culte des héros et ses conditions sociales. Saint Patrick, héros national de l'Irlande*, Paris 1919.

52. 'Sauve-toi de ton sang, pour qu'il ne te tache pas' ('Beware of thy blood, lest it besmirch thee')—forthcoming study.

53. Lévi-Strauss quotes this Andaman myth from E.-H. Man, *On the Aboriginal Inhabitants of the Andaman Islands*, London 1883, pp. 94-5 (*Elementary Structures*, pp. 457 and 497). Jesus's reply to the Sadducees can be found in the Gospels (Matthew 22, 30; Mark 12, 26; Luke 20, 35). In the French translations, it does not evoke the text quoted by E.-H. Man; however, the English translation is close enough to it to justify wondering if this phrase from the Gospels did not influence Man—or the Andaman islanders—at least in the form that has come down to us. But the substance remains authentic, and that is what matters.

(certainly prehistoric), seems to be far less ancient than that of exogamy. Let us also recall its lack of connection with any one race, language, or people, or even with any one civilization; but its manifest connection with a homogeneous, continuous geographical area, which corresponds roughly to the Ancient World, roughly to the oldest spread of the neolithic, and roughly to the region in which procreation is a patriotic duty. Finally, let us recall the very likely association of endogamy with a demographic 'detente', a variation in man's relationship with the space that feeds him; it explains the constant association of endogamy with a natalist, expansionist, 'racist' policy of conquest.[54]

The other hypotheses in this chapter—concerning the origins of *Homo sapiens* and of exogamy—are only attempts at explanation, and unlike the foregoing, are in no way deductions from a long chain of observed facts. Nevertheless, they provisionally fill the gaps left by rather more solid hypotheses, and they are confirmed by the fact that dominates anthropological experience: the astonishing homogeneity of the human species as a whole.[55] I do not, of course, consider as a serious argument the piquancy of the idea that our brains are the result of an invention by the Neanderthal brute, a gift upon which, with all our science, we have been unable to improve.

---

54. The endogamous zone seems to have represented a fairly restricted island in the past, but the civilizations to which it corresponds are in the process of covering the entire globe.

55. All breeders have experience of how easily racial variants may be created within a species, whether naturally or artificially: the Pomeranian (lapdog), for example, is a descendant of real wolves from the Germanic forests, and ten thousand years at most separate it from its wild ancestors. As for the human species, the infant does indeed apparently at first enjoy a potential range of skills that seem to be effectively equivalent in all racial groups. Subsequently—very early on—the environment acts to develop or check these skills, and to differentiate little humans as they move from infancy to childhood.

3

Keeping to Oneself

Incest and Nobility

From Gibraltar to Constantinople, on the sea's northern and southern shores alike, among Christians and Muslims, among town-dwellers and country people, among settled and nomadic populations, there is to this day an enhanced sensitivity, both collective and individual, to a particular ideal of virile brutality and a complementary dramatization of feminine virtue. The two are welded into a notion of family pride that thirsts for blood and extends beyond itself into two myths: ancestry and posterity. The entire paraphernalia is regularly accompanied by what, in sociological jargon, is termed endogamy, which may go as far as incest.

On the African and Asiatic shores of the Mediterranean, there are regions where endogamy is currently practised and others where it is merely desired; in the former we find most of the tribes of large-scale and medium transhumance and the very well established societies of landed peasants, while the latter, until recently, covered the major part of the territory (the major part, but not all, even in the past[1]). Today the change is beyond doubt in the rich, industrialized regions. Elsewhere, it is sometimes simulated. For the past two generations, in fact, it has been possible to meet intellectuals from the Maghreb who reject the old rules and like to claim they are not applied in their own homes, *because they do not want*

---

1. There are regions of Berber-speaking Africa in which traces of exogamy subsist (the Tuareg provinces, and perhaps the Middle and High Atlas and the Ouarsenis). They are very restricted in comparison with the aforementioned and, far away from the frequented areas, appear even more archaic.

to apply them. On the spot, one finds that even the most convincing of them still experience family conflicts between the endogamous tradition and individualism.

As we saw in the last chapter, this desire for endogamy seems connected with an expansionist society, and enables us to define an area of the world opposed, in certain essential structures, to that other hemisphere where, over the past five centuries, the men we call savages were discovered.[2] The latter belong almost exclusively to people unknown to the Ancients; however, if the hypotheses of the last chapter are accepted, this is not pure chance. In fact, to the great surprise of the first theoreticians of ethnology, it quite soon emerged that the more 'primitive' a society was (in the terminology still current today), the more complicated it was. Much stranger still: among these 'savages' and 'primitives', one often finds a manifest irritation at their own complexities and an unsatisfied longing for simplicity.

Among anthropological theories capable of explaining a very wide range of phenomena, there is one that more than any other accords with the perspective of our subject: it is the one Claude Lévi-Strauss put forward in the work he entitled *The Elementary Structures of Kinship*.[3] The author knew better than anyone the contradictions presented by ethnographical investigation, above all when extended to a global scale; that is why he circumscribed his field of study so carefully. To put it simply, the book almost exclusively explores the 'new worlds', such as we have just defined them. Within this framework, Lévi-Strauss analyses the rules of marriage and shows in connection with them that the incest prohibition—a universal phenomenon—is closely linked with the obligation to exchange women, a crucial stage in communication. He defines this wish—or need—to communicate as fundamental, which it undoubtedly is. But communication might be necessary to progress, to civilization, and even to the individual man without on that account corresponding to a *conscious and articulated* will of society. Yet the fact is that exchange of women in 'savage' societies obeys explicit laws. There are other societies, however,

2. See chapter 2.
3. Lévi-Strauss, *Elementary Structures*, pp. 32–3.

which precisely form the object of this study, where the situation is the exact reverse: if exchange is encountered there (as, of course, it is), it occurs *despite* a universally expressed social will.

Prohibition of Exchange

Marriage among certain relatives is now, to be sure, forbidden in the Maghreb. But this rule exists throughout the world, and there are wide differences in its application. When the incest prohibition appears as a 'primitive' fact, it eliminates from the roster of possible spouses a whole category of people, not necessarily relatives according to our lights, but bearing the same name and calling each other 'brother', 'sister'—like the young Vietnamese from the Muong Highlands whose suicide Georges Condominas has recounted, provoked by his shame at having been acknowledged guilty of incest. His partner belonged to his maternal lineage, but was only a thirtieth cousin; moreover, she was a widow, which almost everywhere means 'available'.[4] The prohibition essentially concerned with natural kinship is quite different. It forbids marriage only between very close relatives. What is then involved is a measure inspired by a relatively ancient conception of health or morality, but one we continue to espouse (which, by the way, is why we call it simply Morality).

Well, when one speaks of the Maghreb, one should not lose sight of the fact that our 'morality' has very old roots there; and the Levant is the ground that was its very cradle. We must therefore view our own, present-day ideas as possibly, on occasion, 'archaeological'—by which I mean liable to constitute an element of the subsoil and, as such, then to reappear to us half buried in the dust of centuries. So when, in an archaic environment in the Maghreb, we examine a custom with respect to which the great monotheistic religions have taken a position, we are well advised not to consider it in isolation, but always alongside the religious law of the region; whether this be Christian or Muslim, the mechanism is the same. We then perceive that when religion has taken over a custom that predates it, practice invariably *reinforces* the law. Conversely,

---

4. Georges Condominas, *Nous avons mangé la forêt*, Paris 1957 p. 106.

when religion has opposed custom, the incidence of religious in-fractions will give us the most valuable evidence concerning how deep-rooted the usage in question is.

The Koran, for instance, proclaims that prayer is the first duty of the believer, and places this study even above that of observing the Ramadan fast; from time to time it mentions the veil, but advocates it only for women of the Prophet's family; it makes *no* allusion to circumcision. All Muslims, of course, think that the Koran is a perfect book. Yet we find them, without a single exception, confor-ming to the practice of circumcision—a practice that, in the area in which it is observed today, was already ancient more than a thou-sand years before the birth of the Prophet.[5] We find them—pain-fully—giving up the practice of the veil (likewise older than Islam), and, in large numbers, attaching great importance to fasting. By contrast, they consider themselves good Muslims even though they hardly ever enter the mosque and very often do not even know how to say their prayers.

No social rule is apparently more ancient than the incest prohibi-tion. Yet *in this instance* the practice of the 'noble Mediterranean peoples' continues, even today, to fall short of religious law. Even marriages between an uncle and his niece can be encountered among them, among practising Jews and old Arab Christians in Lebanon as much as among some Muslims. By means of such unions, practised by all Mediterranean minorities, little com-munities ringed by the billows of the great majority religions strive to keep themselves different.

The case reported by Francis Nicolas (among the Tamesna Tuareg) is not of this kind.[6] He writes: 'The sexual prohibition ex-ists between half-brothers and -sisters sharing a father, but not be-tween those having the same mother. A man may marry his pater-nal or maternal aunt; marriage is lawful between first cousins.' In actual fact, this is most probably a misconception. For all Tuareg distinguish between 'cross-cousins' (daughters of maternal uncles or paternal aunts), whom they consider to be in-laws and not

---

5. See p. 82 below, on circumcision and the ban on eating pork.
6. Francis Nicolas, *Tamesna, les Ioullemmeden de l'Est ou Touâreg 'Kel Dînnîk'*, *Cercle de T'âwa. Colonie du Niger*, Paris 1950, p. 213.

relatives, and 'parallel cousins' (daughters of maternal aunts and paternal uncles), whom they call 'sisters' and treat in a brotherly fashion. They do think highly of marriages with a 'sister/cousin', but only on the mother's side, since they disapprove in general of marriages with the *'sister/cousin' on the father's side* (looked on with such favour north of the Sahara, and among Levantine Arabs). Among Tuareg of the Ahaggar region, the imperatives of inheritance sometimes impose a marriage between uncle and niece, or between aunt and nephew; but incest between father and daughter is classified under the heading of 'law-breaking' (which, however, should never be overlooked when studying a society, since depending on the time and place a person may be more or less of a law-breaker for one and the same crime[7]).

Kings of Egypt

Among the ancient Egyptians, before Christianity and before Islam, incest was not only not forbidden, but may even have been motivated by piety or respect for tradition. By way of example, here are a few family details concerning three sovereigns of the Eighteenth Dynasty.[8] Pharaoh Amenôphis III died in the year 1372 BC. The names of several of his wives are known, the favourite among these apparently having been Queen Tiye; he nevertheless married their own daughter Satamon. His eldest son, Amenôphis IV, succeeded him. The new king changed his name upon changing his religion, but is above all known to art-lovers as the husband of the very beautiful Nefertiti. He had several daughters by her, and married the eldest of these (Meritaton) to his brother Smenkhkerē.

---

7. In Djanet around 1950, a religious personage whose practice it was to visit single women in the villages through which he passed in search of alms, inadvertently noticed too late that one of these women was his own daughter: he had to make a charitable donation and apologize, and there was also a public prayer. Equally exceptional was the case of a certain Druze who, in 1925, came to consult a Sheikh in Mascara: 'Is it permitted by religion to eat the apples of a tree one has planted?' 'Yes', the Sheikh replied. The supplicant, reassured by this approval, blithely married his own daughter.

8. Christiane Desroches-Noblecourt, *Tutankhamen. Life and Death of a Pharaoh*, Harmondsworth 1965.

He himself married the youngest, Ankhsenpaton, aged eleven, and by her soon had a 'daughter/granddaughter', Tashery.

In the last period of his life, he seems to have lived apart from his main wife, Nefertiti, but by contrast in a curious intimacy with his 'brother/son-in-law' Smenkhkerē: he had him depicted together with himself, in a pose which many Egyptologists consider to be conjugal, and assigned him one of the forenames initially reserved for Nefertiti.[9] The mummy that experts attribute most convincingly to Smenkhkerē belongs to a twenty-three-year-old prince, a devotee of the cult launched by Amenōphis IV, having the same skull shape as Tutankhamūn—three facts that make the attribution plausible. At all events, the body, which is that of a man, has a quite feminine pelvis and is interred in the sarcophagus of a woman, in the pose of the royal wives: left arm folded over the breast, right arm at the side of the body.

After the death of Amenōphis IV and his 'brother/son-in-law/widow', it was a nine-year-old child and brother to these two who became king, with the name of Tutankhamūn. He was promptly married to his niece and sister-in-law, the little Ankhsenpaton, at once daughter and widow of Amenōphis IV. They had no live child, and when Tutankhamūn died it was his 'widow/niece/sister-in-law' who succeeded him. She had the power to transmit sovereignty, but not to exercise it; so she had to remarry at once, to an old official, the Grand Vizier Ay. Now the latter, it seems, was simultaneously her grandfather and her great-uncle, but this time through the female line. (It is thought, in fact, that Ay was the brother of Tiye, Ankhsenpaton's paternal grandmother, and father of the beautiful Nefertiti, the little queen's mother.)

A thousand years later, we find on the throne of Egypt a Greek family, who reigned for three centuries. All the kings born of this

---

9. In the following pages, the story will be found of a king of Syracuse who married his son to one of his daughters. According to Louis Gernet, the motive for this marriage was to have this son accepted as his successor (he was born of a non-Syracusan mother, whereas the daughters, both of another marriage, were Syracusans on both sides). Well, Amenōphis IV likewise sought to have his brother Smenkhkerē accepted as his successor (in particular, by marrying him to his eldest daughter), and this may explain his strange attitude. The other explanation is the exceptional beauty that portraits of his young brother reveal to us.

line called themselves Ptolemy, and almost all the queens were forenamed Cleopatra. They all, men and women alike, had dramatic lives, which also strike us as criminal, but which were at the same time so strangely similar to one another that the word 'crime' loses all meaning.

The founder of the dynasty, Alexander's comrade-in-arms, was born in Macedonia in the year 360 BC. Despite this European origin, which they all proclaimed, the second king of the dynasty, Ptolemy II, set a fashion to which all his descendants were to remain faithful: upon his ascent to the throne (283 BC), he had two of his brothers murdered and married one of his sisters. His son, Ptolemy III, married only a first cousin and did not kill her. But his grandson, Ptolemy IV, was suspected of having poisoned his father in order to capture power; and upon his accession, in 222 BC, had his mother, his brother, and his sister/wife Arsinoe put to death.

The sixth Ptolemy also married his sister (172 BC), but was obliged to associate his brother and wife with him in the exercise of sovereignty. When he died, twenty-six years later, the fruit of that family union, Ptolemy VII, was proclaimed sole king by his mother. However, he had a paternal uncle—the one whose co-sovereignty his father had accepted—who married the queen mother: in other words, at once his sister and his brother's widow. On the day of the wedding (146 BC), he had his nephew and son-in-law murdered and succeeded him, with the name of Ptolemy VIII—without, it seems, meeting any resistance. Subsequently, he repudiated his sister, which scandalized his subjects. Was it to recover lost prestige that he married his twofold niece (daughter at once of his sister and of his brother)? Or was all this part of a system? The brother and sister were nevertheless reconciled somewhat later, and the king associated one of the sons he had had from this first marriage (Ptolemy IX) to the throne. But it was a son born of his niece who succeeded him, and became the tenth Ptolemy.

Ptolemy X, like his predecessors, married his sister. He was dethroned by his younger brother (Ptolemy XI), but recovered his throne. His sister/wife, Cleopatra, gave him a daughter, and then, having been repudiated, remarried outside the family; a second sister (also called Cleopatra) murdered her. A year later, the second sister was killed by her brother-in-law (the elder one's second husband), and it was a third sister who married the brother/king.

When the latter died, the daughter of one of these sisters reigned and, since she had no brother, married her first cousin, Ptolemy XII.

The latter, a short time after the wedding, had his wife murdered and was put to death by his subjects; he left no child. A natural son of Ptolemy X then took power, under the name of Ptolemy XIII. The people chased him from the throne and replaced him by two of his daughters; when one of these died, he killed the other and recovered his throne. In his will, he bequeathed the crown to his eldest son, Ptolemy XIV, in association with his third daughter. Ptolemy XIV died accidentally before the wedding, but a younger brother, Ptolemy XV, succeeded him, married their sister, and was murdered by her. The latter was named Cleopatra—like her grandmothers and her aunts. She seduced Roman generals, intrigued, governed, died. Unlike the others, she was not forgotten.

Patriarchs of Israel

In Israel, during the epoch described in Genesis, a distinction was made between the father's sister and the mother's sister, the former being seen as a possible wife. Abraham, the holy prophet who engendered the Arabs and Jews, says about his wife Sarah: 'Indeed she is my sister; she is the daughter of my father, but not the daughter of my mother; and she became my wife.'[10] The Old Testament finds this union entirely lawful.[11] By contrast, when it mentions the seduction of Abraham's nephew, the aged Lot, by his two daughters, its approval is not so explicit. Here is the text in question (Genesis 19, 30–38): 'And Lot went up out of Zoar, and dwelt in the mountain, and his two daughters with him; for he feared to dwell in Zoar: and he dwelt in a cave, he and his two daughters. And the first-born said unto the younger: "Our father is old, and there is not a man in the earth to come in unto us after the manner of all the earth. Come, let us make our father drink wine, and we will lie with him, that we may preserve seed of our father." And

10. Genesis 20, 12.
11. Eight centuries later, when Ammon, son of David, violated his half-sister Tamar, the latter reproached him for his violence, saying that he could have asked their father for her (Samuel II, 12, 12). This type of marriage was subsequently forbidden (Leviticus 18, 9 and 20, 17; Deuteronomy 27, 22).

they made their father drink wine that night. And the first-born went in, and lay with her father; and he knew not when she lay down, nor when she arose. And it came to pass on the morrow, that the first-born said unto the younger: "Behold, I lay yesternight with my father. Let us make him drink wine this night also; and go thou in, and lie with him, that we may preserve seed of our father." And they made their father drink wine that night also. And the younger arose, and lay with him; and he knew not when she lay down, nor when she arose. Thus were both the daughters of Lot with child by their father. And the first-born bore a son, and called his name Moab—the same is the father of the Moabites unto this day. And the younger, she also bore a son, and called his name Ben-ammi— the same is the father of the children of Ammon unto this day.'

This story, which we find pretty scandalous, is a little less so when compared with what is revealed about the period's social mores by other passages of Genesis. When Abraham sees his favourite son (the only one he has from the marriage with his sister) attain an age to take a wife, he sends a loyal servant to the land of his birth, there to seek a young virgin born of his paternal lineage. When the steward achieves his aim, he repeats his master's words: 'But thou shalt go unto my father's house, and to my kindred, and take a wife unto my son.'[12] The woman chosen is Rebecca, *granddaughter of Abraham's brother*.

Isaac and Rebecca have twin sons. The eldest, Esau, sells his birthright to the younger, Jacob, and it is the latter who receives the blessing. He is also at once faced with the problem of 'endogamous marriage', for Esau first married two foreign (Hittite) women, of whom his mother says: 'I am weary of my life because of the daughters of Heth.'[13] Moreover, when his brother Jacob sets off for the land of Abraham in order to take a wife there, Esau sees that 'the daughters of Canaan pleased not Isaac his father'.[14] He then visits his uncle Ishmael to seek a third wife, who will be his cousin-german in the male line.

---

12. Genesis 24, 38.
13. Genesis 27, 46.
14. Genesis 28, verses 6, 7, 8 and 9.

Meanwhile, the 'blessed son' Jacob continues his quest within his father's lineage. He arrives in the land of his grandfather Abraham's birth, and finds his maternal uncle, Laban. (This maternal uncle, let us not forget, is the grandson of one of Abraham's brothers: in other words, he is also a paternal uncle.) Jacob serves his uncle for seven years to obtain his cousin Rachel, whom he has loved from the moment he set eyes upon her.[15] On his wedding day, he finds he has been married unwittingly to the elder sister, Leah, and has to serve his uncle for another seven years to win the younger sister.[16]

Indo-European Monarchs

On the other side of the Mediterranean, we find this same distinction between the father's sister and the mother's sister, notably in an episode from the life of a tyrant in the fifth century BC: Dionysius the Elder. He had married two wives on the same day, both of noble birth; but one was a native of Syracuse, while the other came from some foreign city. Now, it was the foreign woman who bore a son, while the Syracusan gave birth to two daughters. Louis Gernet has noted a series of concordant traditions that suggest that the tyrant's daughters, because of their mother's Syracusan nationality, seemed to contemporaries to be more 'legitimate' than his son. In the event, Dionysius the Younger did indeed succeed his father, but *against the will of his future subjects*.[17] To

---

15. Jacob 'pays' his uncle with seven years' service, but when the uncle marries off his daughters he gives each of them a 'handmaid' (which may be translated 'slave'). Genesis 29, 24.

16. Genesis 29: 22, 25, and 26: 'And Laban gathered together all the men of the place, and made a feast.... And it came to pass in the morning that, behold, it was Leah; and he said to Laban: "What is this thou hast done unto me? did not I serve with thee for Rachel? wherefore then hast thou beguiled me?" And Laban said: "It is not so done in our country , to give the younger before the first-born."' We may note in this connection that the country in question stretches to the Atlantic. I have known personally many contemporary 'Labans' in the Maghreb, where, to this day, it is contrary to custom to settle a younger daughter before the elder. The Old Testament, moreover, is full of precepts designed to oblige young women and men to have as many children as they can.

17. Louis Gernet, 'Marriages de tyrans', in *Hommage à Lucien Febvre*, Paris 1954, vol. 2, pp. 41–2.

cut a long story short, when his children grew up, Dionysius the Elder married his eldest daughter to his son, perhaps to justify the latter's claims to the throne. As for his younger daughter, he married her off to his brother; she became a widow and remarried, this time wedding her maternal uncle. 'In Athens, and no doubt in many parts of Greece, one could marry one's father's sister (though not one's mother's sister): we know instances of it. One might also marry one's niece: in particular, marriage with one's brother's daughter was not merely permitted, but was viewed with a certain favour, even in the classical epoch. In material from legend, it appears with significant frequency. In family law, it had the status of an institution: if a deceased man left only a daughter, she was normally taken as wife (under the name Epiclaira) by her father's nearest relative—her father's brother being looked to first.'[18]

The pharaohs of the Eighteenth Dynasty and the tyrants of Sicily were historical personages. More uncertain, though more recent, is the information we possess regarding the ancient Irish. Strabo tells us that they were even more savage than the Britons, 'since they are man-eaters as well as herb-eaters, and since, further, they count it an honourable thing, when their fathers die, to devour them, and openly to have intercourse, not only with the other women, but also with their mothers and sisters.' He adds: 'I am saying this only with the understanding that I have no trustworthy witnesses for it...'[19] Strabo is actually referring here to Pytheas, of whom he says elsewhere: 'Pytheas [has] been found, upon scrutiny, to be an arch-falsifier.'[20] However, the main hero of Irish epic, King Cúchulainn, was born of the incestuous union of King Conchobhar with his sister Deirdriu.[21] As for Clothru, sister of the Queen of Connaught Medhbh (prototype of Queen Mab), she had triplet brothers who fought their father for the kingship of Ireland. 'Before the battle, she bore to the three of them a son, whom she married.'[22]

18. Ibid., p. 44.
19. *The Geography of Strabo*, London 1923 (Loeb Classics), vol. 2, pp. 259–60 (Bk 4.5.4).
20. Ibid., vol. 1, p. 235 (Bk 1.4.3).
21. Czarnowski,*Culte des héros*, p. 262.
22. Hubert, *Greatness and Decline of the Celts*, p. 203.

I have not searched systematically for all the historical or semi-historical examples of incest to be found in the Ancient World, but have simply mentioned the first that came into my head. The important point is that before Christianity and before Islam, incest was a practice that did not have the sacrilegious character in this region of the world that exogamous peoples attribute to it. And even in our own day, despite Islam and despite Christianity, marriages these two religions forbid or advise against—between niece and uncle (particularly on the father's side), or between nephew and aunt—are still relatively numerous.[23]

A French survey, carried out on 3,450,000 Catholic marriages solemnized between 1946 and 1958, reveals that 253 dispensations were granted for the celebration of a union between an uncle and his niece or between an aunt and her nephew—not a very large figure for a country in which such marriages are accepted, but an incredible figure in a part of the world where such marriages are seen as scandalous.[24] The number of civil weddings celebrated in France between such close relatives is not known, and the number of 'common-law marriages' still less so. It would, moreover, be interesting to note the number of cases of incest between father and daughter that arrive before the courts in Europe. It would also be interesting to compare the sentences meted out by juries for this sort of crime. People who know their own district well have assured me that peasant jurors were far more indulgent than those who came from towns; these same people can all cite several cases of incest, in their own villages, that have escaped the eye of justice. In certain regions of France (such as the area watered by the upper Loire and the Rhône), the attention of ecclesiastical observers has been drawn to the number of cases of daughters being deflowered by their fathers. A Swiss psychiatrist has told me of the same

23. Among the Tuareg, two such marriages took place in a single family (a noble one, it is true). They are, however, considered by Islam generally as a grave sin and are explicitly forbidden by the Koran. See Michel Vallet, 'Généalogie des Kel Ghela' (unpublished paper for the Sixth Section of the École Pratique des Hautes Études).

24. Jean Sutter and Jean-Michel Goux, 'Évolution de la consanguinité en France de 1926 à 1958, avec des données récentes détaillées', Population, 1962, no. 4, pp. 693–700; Jean Sutter and Claude Levy, 'Les dispenses civiles au mariage en France depuis 1800', Population, 1959, no. 2, pp. 299–302.

phenomenon in the Valais. This may, of course, be put down to alcoholism, but alcoholism is rife elsewhere. Here we are still in the domain of the unusual and even scandalous—a scandal, however, that has greater juridical importance in towns than in the countryside.

Keeping the Girls in the Family for the Boys in the Family

Moving from the exceptional to everyday practice, we find that almost everywhere in the Maghreb, and in the greater part of the Levant, even today the 'ideal marriage' takes place with the female relative who, while not a sister, most resembles one. In practice, of course, the 'sister' in question is a first cousin, daughter of a paternal uncle.[25] But it is precisely the cousin for whom, in Tuareg (the best preserved Berber dialect), the *only* old appellation is 'my sister'. Everywhere else in the Maghreb, a confected word of Arabic origin serves to designate this very close relative—*bint 'ammi, oult-'ammi,* which means literally 'daughter of my paternal uncle'—but in songs, in the language of love, and even in daily usage, female cousins are usually spoken of as 'my sisters', 'my sister'.[26] The custom of using these terms of kinship has even entered so deeply into popular manners that, when the Algerian War supervened to exalt the ideal bond of camaraderie, those in the underground did not call each other 'comrade' (as we did under oppression in France), but 'sister', 'brother'. At a level less noble but still quite instructive to observe, since heavily marked by Corsican, Sicilian, and Algerian influences—I allude to the French social layer known as the *milieu*—women who walk the streets to support pimps are known by the latter as 'sisters'. And among themselves

---

25. Part of chapter 5 ('Lo, Our Wedding-feast Is Come, O my Brother') is devoted to marriage between cousins.

26. Same practice among the inhabitants of the Levant. See A. Aymard and J. Auboyer, *L'Orient et la Grèce antique*, Paris 1963, p. 48: 'In Egyptian poetry, the young man calls his lover "my sister" and she in turn calls him "my brother". The same was true in everyday usage between husband and wife. Does this mean that consanguineous marriage was the rule? Some people think so, others deny it. The former point out that Egyptian mythology, with Osiris and Isis, offered a prestigious example of it.'

tramps, just like the most primitive peoples, call themselves simply 'men'.

Accompanying this quest for a union with the nearest female relative, we find in these same regions of the Mediterranean traces of a very ancient desire *not to communicate*: to keep all the girls in the family for the boys in the family; to link oneself by marriage to an alien lineage only under the pressure of some compelling necessity. To live in close proximity with people to whom one is not bound by ties of consanguinity and even legal kinship (for uterine relatives are, in many places, barely tolerated) is a source of humiliation. So every resource of trickery and violence is almost invariably mustered to prevent outsiders from establishing themselves on a stable basis in the neighbourhood. The logical corollary of such a state of mind is the adoption 'as a relative' of the neighbour one has not managed to get rid of.

It seems clear that the situation in the Maghreb is exactly the opposite of that described by all ethnologists who have observed the 'savage' hemisphere. This inverse parallelism, moreover, is as close as can be: for whereas in the New Worlds the taboo forbidding marriage between individuals from the same encampment or lineage, or bearing the same name, often extends to diet, everywhere in the Old World we find traces of the repugnance inspired by foreign food.

Eating Meat From One's Herd Is Like Marrying a Paternal Uncle's Daughter

An old Moroccan scholar, a man of great learning and fine judgement with whom I was discussing the predilection in the Maghreb for 'marriage within the family', cited an opinion he considered general, summarizing it this way: 'People like to marry the daughter of their paternal uncle, just as they like to eat meat of their own breeding' (literally: slaughter an animal from their herd).[27] To sensitive towndwellers reading this, the word 'slaughter' (*égorger*) conjures up the image of a bloody act. But for

---

27. The saying can also be understood in the opposite sense, as meaning that people shrink from marrying a cousin just as they shrink from raiding their own herd.

nomads and peasants, slaughter means above all 'a good meal, a feast at which you eat meat'—a great feast when a sheep or even an ox is killed, a lesser feast when only a chicken or two is sacrificed. In the High Atlas, I have even heard the Berber word meaning 'a feast with meat' translated by a French neologism that I have never come across elsewhere: *une égorgette*.[28] In French, the expression is surprising, since the root *égorger* strikes fear into the imagination, while the feminine diminutive suffix-*ette* evokes some little, pretty, gay, dainty thing. But as it stands, this bizarre term, of popular origin, perfectly translates the word in the original language; everything of the Berber, right up to the final *t* denoting the feminine or a diminutive, is reproduced in the adaptation, with—by a strange coincidence—the same meaning in both languages.

In the Maghreb, more frequently than elsewhere, one encounters a range of feelings that have no official designation, although no individual is entirely unacquainted with them. Among these may be classified the deep love and internal peace procured by surroundings and objects where nothing is unfamiliar, where no threat of a human nature is to be anticipated, but there is also a place for the suburbanite's simple delight in the fruits of his own orchard, vegetables from his garden. This naive joy restores to us the proud satisfaction of all the old owners of land in the Ancient World, as they savour wine from their vineyards, water from their springs,[29] bread baked at home by the women of the family out of wheat the father has harvested from his own land, with the help of his younger brothers and his sons (some peasants from the Maghreb claim to recognize its taste).

---

28. In Berber, feminine singular: *thamghrout*; plural: *thimghras* (from *ghars*: to slaughter, or slit the throat of).

29. In Bombay, I was once lucky enough to become acquainted with two Indian women brought up in Paris, then married to brahmins and provided with mothers-in-law. They spoke to me, in particular, of the dietary taboos they had to watch out for: a brahmin who goes on a journey even takes his own water with him (the water of his own well); and all food that is not 'home-produced' disgusts him, whether it is forbidden or not. 'But Jacquemont, in India, when he watched his Sepoys feeding, saw as many stoves, pots, fires, and cooking [techniques] as there were men. No two of them would eat together, or of the same food.' Lucien Febvre, *A Geographical Introduction to History*, London 1925, p. 167.

Happiness at keeping all one's children near, held fast by husbands and wives of their own blood; pride at being well defended by their solidarity and numbers—I often heard these sentiments expressed in pre-1940 peasant Algeria. One is inevitably reminded of this other proverb, from a different universe:

Your own mother,
Your own sister,
Your own pigs,
Your own yams that you have piled up,
You may not eat.
Other people's mothers,
Other people's sisters,
Other people's pigs,
Other people's yams that they have piled up,
You may eat.[30]

Margaret Mead, who records this aphorism, points out that the forbidden yams are only those used for seed. Obviously! For where one must exchange one cannot exchange everything, any more than everything can be kept where the desire is to preserve. But the will to exchange is as clearly expressed by the proverb from Oceania as the contrary will seems to me to be expressed in the everyday life of the Maghreb. And in both cases, will is what we are talking about.

---

30. Mead, *Sex and Temperament*, p. 83. (Lévi-Strauss used this text as sub-title to Part One of *Elementary Structures*: see p. 27.)

4

The Maghreb in the Butter Age

In the Beginning Was a Continuation

In North Africa as elsewhere, however far back one goes into the racial past of modern man, one finds a *mixture*. What is unusual about the Maghreb is that the mixture of anthropological types discernible today is made up of elements analogous—let us be clear: close, but not identical—to those that prehistoric excavations have made it possible to reconstruct for the epoch known as Capsian, from six to eight thousand years ago.[1] They include various types, some black and of unknown provenance,[2] others of the so-called Mediterranean type, and others again, the most numerous, recalling Cro-Magnon man.[3] It is likely that the present-day inhabitants

1. The Capsian drew its name and definition from Gafsa in Tunisia. Although related to the European Aurignacian, it was certainly later: probably contemporary with the Magdalenian, which it does not resemble. Capsian industry is to be found throughout the continental Maghreb, in East Africa (Kenya), and, sporadically, in the Sahara. It is, moreover, not inconceivable that from the end of the Capsian the Sahara was traversed by people influenced by the already neolithic civilization that was invading Egypt from the Mediterranean Levant during this period. In 1939, in the heart of the Aurès, I excavated a rock-covered shelter belonging to the Capsian industry. (My notes, unfortunately, were never published, since they disappeared with my other papers after my arrest by the Gestapo in 1942.)

2. Henriette Alimen, *The Prehistory of Africa*, London 1957, p. 340: 'There are, however, in the Capsian levels some skeletons with negroid affinities.'

3. He owes his name to a little village in the department of the Dordogne, where his remains were identified for the first time. We are dealing not with a 'race', but with a type apparently universal at a certain stage of human evolution. Early prehistorians, not incorrectly, found traces of him almost everywhere; but from this they deduced improbable 'racial' migrations.

of the Maghreb are still descended from that varied Capsian stock, so it is appropriate to say a few words about it.

The men of the Capsian used tools of cut stone, so they belong to palaeolithic civilization; but they lived six or seven thousand years ago, and were therefore contemporary with the beginnings of the neolithic. Physically they were widely differentiated, but they had in common a way of life, one that bore no relation to that of their descendants, since they had no knowledge of cereal crops or of domestic animals, and fed themselves poorly with whatever hunting or gathering might bring in. They manufactured little flints (not very well shaped) and bone needles.[4] They used ostrich eggs (no doubt for carrying water). They sometimes lived in caves, where they built fires and ate huge quantities of snails, whose empty shells may be found in enormous heaps mixed with ashes. We also know that they used to pull out two upper incisors, and we believe they used to paint their bodies red (since ground pigments have been found in some of their deposits).

If, when travelling through the Aurès mountains, you see a cavity in the rock not too far from a trickle of water, dig a narrow trench there. You will find, first of all, traces of occupancy by Shawiya pastors: they will have left a few ashes, date-stones, and easily identifiable potsherds. Under a layer of sand, you will again find ashes and very probably a few shards of Roman pottery; then, under the Roman ashes, more sand in a thick layer. Finally there comes a deep level, in which the men of the Capsian tell us their secrets: here I have found small, poorly fashioned flints, a few fragments of ostrich-egg shell, a bone needle, and thousands of snail shells buried in an enormous mass of ashes, the thickest of the three.

The Soup Civilization

However, while the inhabitants of the Maghreb were still hunting their snails, an extraordinary event was under way somewhere west

---

4. No doubt other needles too, made out of thorns, which have not survived to our day. Acacia thorns are as hard as steel, and some are also as long as a man's finger. I have seen Tuareg manufacturing a needle with two thorns, using one to pierce the other.

of the Caspian Sea and the River Indus. This extraordinary event was the birth of civilization: that is to say, essentially, the invention of agriculture and stock-rearing and the birth of urban life. Agriculture (meaning bread), stock-rearing (butter and milk), pottery (a soup-bowl): such were the three major gifts the Mediterranean Levant bestowed upon humanity.

The first true civilization, that of soup, very quickly spread westward.[5] When it reached the Maghreb, it transformed the pattern of life radically;[6] and the Snail-eaters forthwith adopted the type of diet, mode of living, and seasonal rhythm that they generally retained up to the beginning of the twentieth century. But although they had become farmers and herdsmen, they did not therefore renounce the free gifts of nature: collecting chestnuts or sweet acorns; game. So at Teniet-el-Had in 1955, in the gathering season, I saw acorns being sold at 2,000 francs a quintal; in the same place and year, barley at the grocer's cost 450-500 francs for twenty litres, in other words the same price. A survey carried out in Greater Kabylia around 1885 estimated consumption of game by a family of five (father, mother, and three children aged seventeen, ten, and six) at eighty kilograms a year, out of a total meat consumption of 234 kilograms. It may be noted, on the one hand, that game represents a good third of the family's meat consumption, and on the other that this consumption was very much higher eighty years ago than today for the Algerian peasant. Yet even then the author was pointing out that Kabylia 'does not produce half the food needed by its inhabitants'.[7]

The imbalance between the size of the Kabyle population and the resources of its territory has worsened enormously since 1885.

---

5. The transistor civilization took less than ten years to conquer a far vaster area, extending over practically the entire world.

6. Thanks to Carbon 14, scientists have been able to establish that some corn discovered in an Egyptian silo from the neolithic period was reaped between 4600 and 4250 BC (Georges Posener, *A Dictionary of Egyptian Civilization*, London 1962, p. 221, column 1). The same procedure, applied to pieces of charcoal from the upper Capsian of Dra Mta el Abiod (Algeria), gave 5050 BC, give or take 200 years (Alimen, p. 68). (One twentieth of the time-span involved is usually accepted as the margin of error in estimates arrived at by means of Carbon 14 dating.)

7. Auguste Geoffroy, *Bordier, fellah, berbère de la Grande Kabylie*, Paris 1888, p. 78.

Before 1830, a balance must have existed between the population and resources, roughly maintained by infant mortality, war, periodic famines, and voluntary emigration. In this period, meat consumption was probably even higher than in 1885, since game stocks (which always decrease with the rise of human population density) were undoubtedly more abundant. Moreover, we know for sure—in particular through the research of André Nouschi[8]—that Algerian livestock has shrunk a great deal during the past hundred years, as a result of the land confiscations of the colonial epoch. In the period when tribal wars were raging, we must add to the foregoing causes a voluntary tendency to favour herds at the expense of fields, the former being easier to protect from an enemy and, in case of flight, capable of being more readily sheltered from harm. In conclusion, all the information I have (in particular from oral sources) confirms this high level of meat consumption by the Maghreb's inhabitants in a relatively recent past (within the past century).[9]

Such gifts of nature nevertheless ceased to be the sole resource and became a supplement, albeit a highly valued one. The basis of diet henceforth came to be the girdle-cake of barley or wheat, boiled cereals, ewe's milk and butter, kid's flesh. So fundamental a change affects absolutely all activities, and is enough to modify a physical type,[10] without it being necessary to explain such modifications by assuming an influx of new blood. What is more, the 'soup civilization' did not arrive in North Africa of its own accord: men from the Orient brought it in their baggage. However, like those who one day were to bring the Koran, they were not very numerous. Moreover, if we are to believe anthropological or linguistic evidence, they already may have had affinities with the inhabitants of the country. In short, the modification this contribution of new blood effected in the Maghreb's genetic capital was

8. A. Nouschi, *Enquêtes sur le niveau de vie des populations constantinoises de la conquête jusqu'en 1919*, Paris 1961.
9. We may mention in this regard that the relative suppression of milk and meat in today's standard diet—a result, in North Africa, of sedentarization, pauperization, it matters little what medical label we attach to the scourge—is a disaster for the subcontinent's public health.
10. See note 11, chapter 2.

probably of the same order as that which resulted from the Arab invasion: limited. But the revolution in beliefs and customs, for its part, must have been immense, even then.

The Maghreb's First Ethnographer

Three or four thousand years after the snail-eaters, excavations disclose (this time precisely) the present-day anthropological types of the Maghreb,[11] 'anthropological types' denoting *the same human stocks living in the same conditions.* They are herdsmen, they work the land, they bury their dead near huge standing stones, more or less as Europeans began to do a few centuries earlier, doubtless under an influence that reached both of them from the Mediterranean Levant. Apart from this, what do the inhabitants of the Maghreb do with their free time? How are they organized? What do they think? We shall find we have a certain amount of material to help us picture this, for we are dealing with the Mediterranean basin, in other words, the oldest of 'historical zones'.

The first historical references to the Maghreb are found in Egyptian inscriptions back in the earliest dynasties, almost 3,000 years before our era.[12] But they are very poor in descriptive detail of a non-conventional kind, and it is not until the fifth century BC that we have, at last, an 'ethnographical' description. The first ethnographer of the Maghreb was a Greek: Herodotus. This true man of science, inquisitive and honest, was also the very model of the kind of reporter sociologists cherish: scrupulous enough to repeat accurately even what he does not understand or considers absurd, but not so credulous as has been claimed. 'For my part', he says, 'I neither put entire faith in this story ... nor wholly disbelieve

---

11. '...at Roknia, there occur types resembling those of extant Kabyle, Negro and Egyptian populations' (Alimen, p. 403). Roknia is an immense megalithic necropolis (3,000 dolmens) twelve kilometres from Constantine.

12. Under the Fourth Dynasty (2723-2563 BC), King Snofru organized a war expedition against his western neighbours, and apparently brought back eleven thousand prisoners and thirteen thousand head of cattle (Étienne Drioton and Jacques Vandier, *L'Égypte*, Paris 1962, p. 170).

it.'[13] 'I merely record the current story, without guaranteeing the truth of it. It may, however, be true enough.'[14] Through Herodotus, for the first time, we shall at last learn something about the customs and character of these mysterious men from before history, in rather greater detail than that afforded us by the austere secrets of prehistoric kitchen scraps.

They Were Practising Circumcision a Thousand Years Before the Birth of the Prophet

Herodotus, who lived almost a thousand years before the birth of the prophet Muhammad, travelled widely, especially in Egypt. He informs us, among other things, that Egyptian priests regularly shaved their entire bodies; that they carried out four ablutions daily;[15] that all Egyptians had a horror of pork;[16] and that they had practised circumcision since earliest times: 'The Colchians, the Egyptians and the Ethiopians are the only races which from ancient times have practised circumcision. The Phoenicians and the Syrians of Palestine themselves admit that they adopted the practice from Egypt.'[17] The prohibition against eating pork (to be confirmed by the Koran a thousand years later) was probably far older than the entire duration of history, for excavations from the neolithic epoch in Middle Egypt have uncovered deposits revealing: '...cattle and sheep bones in plenty, but no remains of pig. That animal was, however, plentiful in the contemporary settlements in the Fayum and on the Delta's edge.'[18]

We know that no man considers himself an adherent of Islam if he is not circumcised—to the point that in North Africa 'circumcision' is often translated as 'baptism'. It is less well known that the Koran maintains a strange silence concerning this custom, which

---

13. Herodotus, *The Histories*, Harmondsworth 1982, Book Four, 96.
14. *Histories*, Book Four, 195.
15. *Histories*, Book Two, 37.
16. *Histories*, Book Four, 186.
17. *Histories*, Book Two, 104.
18. Childe, *Man Makes Himself*, p. 96. In Blackman's *The Fellahin of Upper Egypt* there will be found an entire chapter devoted to comparing the practices of Antiquity with those still current (pp. 280-316). Reading this, one can only be struck by how conservative this society is (though probably no more than others).

seems so important a thousand years later or a thousand years earlier, for it does not mention it a single time.[19] There is a similar reticence in regard to the Muslim calender: we find that no festival is dedicated to the commemoration of any circumcision whatsoever. Christians have adopted precisely the opposite attitude, for they piously celebrate the anniversary of Jesus's circumcision, but refrain from circumcising their own sons. Now, Christianity's will to universality, and its implantation in Rome, assuredly lay behind the abandonment of circumcision by the first Christians, and the whole matter was one of the reasons for the break between Christianity and Judaism. So what is involved is an important conflict, which had considerable and lasting repercussions throughout the Mediterranean world, and particularly in the very region where the prophet Muhammad lived and preached.

Different in this respect from the religion of Israel (which owes its essentially national and even racial character to its distant origins), Islam, like Christianity, aspired from the outset to be universal. In these conditions, it is difficult not to consider quite deliberate the absolute silence maintained by the Muslims' holy book regarding the ancient Semitic obligation to circumcise male children. And how can we avoid viewing the rigorous fidelity to that practice among all followers of the Koran as not a dogma but a contingency? 'It so happens' that Christianity was preached very early on at Rome, among the uncircumcised, while Islam continued to develop in a Semitic milieu where, as we have just seen, circumcision was already an ancient and general practice more than a thousand years before the coming of the prophet Muhammad.

West of Egypt, an Almost Unknown Land

Herodotus possessed less direct information concerning the immense region that we call the Maghreb and the Hellenic world then termed Libya (it was the Egyptians, the first literate people to encounter the area, who long before the Greeks gave the name *Lebou*

---

19. Of course, numerous authors accepted within Islam as authoritative prescribe circumcision; but it still remains true that the one revealed book, cornerstone of all Muslim doctrine, refrains from so much as mentioning it.

or *Libou* to their western neighbours). Despite this lack of direct knowledge, his physical description of the country is accurate. Herodotus locates the desert correctly, locates likewise the high chain of mountains that stretches parallel to the sea, and enumerates with precision the wild animals that inhabit them. It is not surprising that he should be very well informed about the Greeks and Phoenicians already established along the coast. But he also tells us of the hinterland, populated by natives of whom he says that some are 'Libyans' and others 'Ethiopians', in other words, black. He does not describe the Libyans physically, but the Egyptians portrayed them a thousand years before Herodotus (sometimes with blue eyes, a brown beard, a ruddy complexion). On the other hand, he gives us numerous details concerning their habits, details some of which are often so strangely modern that I think it is worth itemizing them: behind the swift pulsation of events, they will help us discern the slow, slow rhythms of evolution.

In particular, Herodotus informs us that the Libyans eat meat and drink milk as other men do, but like Egyptians refuse to consume or raise pigs.[20] Regarding Libyan dwellings, the ancient author tells us they 'are made of the dry haulms of some plant, knit together with rush ropes', and that they are portable.[21] Similar constructions, using neither stone nor brick nor fabric, can still be found today throughout the eastern Sahara. They are light, cool, well adapted to the country: I have lived in them in the Libyan desert and seen them in Tuareg encampments, among the Toubbou and the Dawada.[22] Called *akabar* (plural: *ikbran*) in Tuareg and *Zarība* in Arabic, nowadays they are rarely moved. But it is certain that nomadism in Africa preceded the introduction of the black tent, so—before this innovation—the portable dwelling Herodotus describes may correspond to the *akabar*. As for the tent of matting so characteristic of the nomads of Niger, it corresponds still better to Herodotus's description and is identical with the *mapalia*

---

20. *Histories*, Book Four, 186.
21. *Histories*, Book Four, 191.
22. 'Dawada' comes from an Arabic plural meaning 'eaters of worms'.

described by Sallust.[23] It is not possible to find it today in Libya or the Ahaggar, for its manufacture requires a raw material lacking in this area: a certain palm-tree (common in the Aïr), the *doum,* called also 'Pharaoh's palm'. However, it is not impossible that *doum* matting, very light and sturdy, was formerly transported over greater distances than today.

The Greek historian points out the simultaneous presence in Libya of two modes of production that still characterize the Maghreb: that of nomadic herdsmen, and that of sedentary agriculturists. He shows us the nomads setting off each year for the date harvest, and mentions the Libyan practice of grilling and eating locusts. He describes how the ancestors of the Maghreb's inhabitants swore oaths by placing their hand upon the tombs of their great men; practised divination by going to sleep on these tombs to dream prophetic dreams; pledged their faith in pacts of brotherhood;[24] solemnly paraded a young girl before a ritual battle during which other girls divided into two camps and fought with sticks and stones.[25] I myself have been present, in the Aurès, at an oath on the tombs;[26] at the ritual parading of a little girl in fields about to be ploughed; at the jousting with sticks and stones of the Kora, on the first day of spring.[27] Date harvesting is still customary for nomads in Mauritania; and as for pacts of brotherhood, they have been described to me—in the High and Middle Atlas, in Kabylia—as something still practised a generation ago.

---

23. The excellent ethnographer Charles Le Coeur (killed in Italy during the Second World War) had observed the matting tent among the Toubbou and on the southern fringes of the Sahara, and thought it corresponded to the very precise description of the *mapalia* to be found in Sallust. See too Georges Marcy, *A propos de Mapalia*, Rabat 1942, p. 23; Emile Laoust, *L'habitation chez les transhumants du Maroc central*, Rabat 1935, pp. 18, 19, and 76; C.-G. Feilberg, *La tente noire*, Copenhagen 1944.

24. *Histories*, Book Four, 172.

25. *Histories*, Book Four, 180.

26. Marceau Gast in *Alimentation des Kel Ahaggar* (unpublished doctoral thesis) notes that in periods of famine old women interrogate tomb-monuments (*idebnan*) to find out when the caravan bringing the millet will arrive.

27. The Kora is a ritual game which is found throughout the Hamitic area: *takourt* in the Aurès, *takerikera* among the Tuareg.

Female Fashions, a Model of Constancy

'I think too', says the old historian, 'that the crying of women at religious ceremonies also originated in Libya—for the Libyan women are much addicted to this practice, and they do it very beautifully.'[28] In this respect the inhabitants of the Maghreb have not changed, and if a contemporary of the circular tombs were to be reborn one wedding day in any North African country, he would doubtless recognize the ululations of his female descendants.

Contrary to what might logically be presumed, female dress too would surprise him very little: colour and cut, it seems, are quite astonishingly constant. This is what Herodotus tells us: 'Libyan women wear goatskins (*aigai*) with the hair stripped off, dyed red and fringed at the edges, and it was from these skins that we took our word "aegis".'[29] According to people I questioned in the Aurès, women's apparel two or three generations ago was made up of a rectangle of garnet-red wool, unsewn and handwoven, which they used to wear directly over a long chemise. The dress observed by Jeanne Jouin in the Kerkenna Islands, moreover, apparently bore a close resemblance to that described to me: 'The women of the Kerkenna islands wear...a rectangular shawl of thick embroidered red woollen fabric'; only one tint is allowed: dark red;[30] the Kerkenna shawl belonging to the Musée de l'Homme collection, illustrated in Jouin's article, is also adorned with fringes. In Tuareg territory around 1939, Dag Ghali slaves were still wearing hide garments dyed red and adorned with fringes.[31] A century earlier, on the other hand, noble Tuareg were already wearing the imported clothes—white, black, or dyed in 'Guinea' blue—by which Europe was to know them shortly afterwards.

'Along the coast to the westward the neighbours of the Nasamones are the Macae. These people wear their hair in the form of a crest, shaving it close on either side of the head and letting it grow

---

28. *Histories*, Book Four, 190.
29. *Histories*, Book Four, 189.
30. Jeanne Jouin, 'Le Tarf des Kerkéniennes', *Revue des Études Islamiques*, 1948, p. 51.
31. Guy Barrère, a schoolteacher in the Ahaggar, has a tunic made of goat and sheep skins tanned in the Aïr and dyed red, manufactured in 1956 or 1957 by an old Dag Ghali woman: it has fringes.

long in the middle.'[32] The Tuareg have only a single word to denote both a cock's comb and this hair style: the word *agharkouba* (plural: *igharkoubaten*). But young children have their hair cut in this fashion in numerous parts of the Maghreb. Throughout Algeria, the untranslatable word *gettaya* is used, as is sometimes also the word *shusha*, to designate either a lock of hair around which the head is shaven, or a hairy strip shaped like a crest. Both are credited with extraordinary protective virtue.[33]

Headless Men and Dog-Headed Men

Even the fables recorded by Herodotus have a familiar ring. For example: 'the region to the west [of the river Triton] is very hilly, and abounds with forest and animal life. It is here that the huge snakes are found—and lions, elephants, bears, asps, and horned asses, not to mention dog-headed men, headless men with eyes in their breasts (I don't vouch for this, but merely repeat what the Libyans say).'[34] Well, when I was collecting tribal genealogies in the Aurès,[35] a family head told me the story of his great-uncle's pilgrimage to Mecca:[36] 'a real pilgrimage', he told me, 'on foot through the desert'. On his way, the pious traveller had met 'the great snakes who eat people, the wild men who go naked; and above all the Beni-Kleb, of whom he recounted on his return: 'They have the smell, fur, and ears of a dog; their hands, face, and feet

---

32. *Histories*, Book Four, 175.

33. El Bokhari, *L'authentique tradition Musulmane, choix de h'adiths*, Paris 1964, pp. 89 and 291, para. 67: 'According to 'Omar ben Nâfi, Ibn 'Omar says he heard God's Messenger (to whom blessing and good health) forbid the *qazà*. When, says 'Obaîd Allah (the previous rawî), I asked ('Omar) what the *qazà* was, he told us by means of gestures (that Nâfi', his father, had said): It is when the child's head is shaven leaving a "tuft of hair" in places, and 'Obaîd Allah again showed his lock of hair and the two sides of his head. As 'Obaîd was asked if this applied equally to (pubescent) girls and boys, he replied: I do not know, for Nâfi' spoke thus: "the child", and yet I asked him once again and he replied: As for the locks on the temples and nape, there is no harm in letting the young man keep these, but the *qazà* (in question) consists in leaving patches of hair alone upon the head. It is the same whether one parts the hair on one side of the head or the other.'

34. *Histories*, Book Four, 192.

35. Between 1934 and 1940.

36. Probably around 1850.

are like a man's.' Manifestly, in the eyes of his great-nephew, it was the encounter with the Beni-Kleb (Herodotus's dog-headed men) that at once proved the truth of his uncle's itinerary, and not the latter's testimony that proved the existence of these strange two-legged creatures.

In another distant corner of the Maghreb—at Ideles, a small agricultural centre in the Ahaggar—a tradition is encountered concerning an itinerant marabout from the Tazrouk region, who died some fifty years ago after having lived among the black men beyond the Hausa country: 'among the cannibals, the Beni A'ryan who live stark naked, and the Beni Kelboun' (a tribe in which all males are born dogs but children of the female sex are women, and the two marry only each other).[37]

For our part, if the almost contemporary testimony of the Tuareg marabout and the Shawiya pilgrim are not sufficient, we may turn to Guillaume le Testu, a Frenchman of the sixteenth century and pilot by profession, author of an atlas wherein he depicted three camels alongside headless men and dog-headed men.[38] Or we may turn to an English knight who is certainly no compiler of second-hand reports, but describes what he has seen: 'towards the South there live people of an ugly and evil nature, who have no heads'.[39] Or we may turn to a priest, a papal envoy to the same regions in the same period, who describes 'people who have faces like dogs'.[40] Or finally, we may turn to the Burgundian sculptor of the great door at Vézelay, who portrays the whole thing on the spandrel of the narthex, flanking the figure of Christ in Majesty. It is even true that, according to one tradition, a dog-headed man was canonized.[41]

Of course, it is not inconceivable that the Greek Herodotus fathered all these tales, for his books were copied, translated,

---

37. I am indebted for this information to Guy Barrère, who speaks Tuareg and for the past eight years has run the school in this little village of sedentary agriculturists, located in the heart of the Ahaggar.

38. Towards 1550.

39. Jean de Mandeville, author of the *Livre de Merveilles*, the manuscript of which was written in French. He travelled between 1332 and 1356.

40. Friar Odrio of Friuli travelled around 1314.

41. 'Saint Christopher, that valiant martyr of Christ, was, we are told, dog-headed' (Émile Mâle, *L'art au XIIe siècle*, Paris 1947, p. 330). A dog-headed St Christopher can be seen among the sculptures in Notre-Dame-de-Paris.

widely disseminated, and may have become 'folklore'.[42] But it is not inconceivable, either, that what was already being recounted in Herodotus's day has gone on being recounted in the same places. At all events, the two anecdotes—the one from the Aurès and the one from the Ahaggar—were by no means considered legends by the people who put them about, but rather as real, recent, indubitable adventures, which had occurred to men universally respected in their villages. 'I merely record the current story, without guaranteeing the truth of it.'

A Huge Pile of Empty Shells

The aim of this somewhat lengthy introduction was not just to situate the first historian relative to his more modern successors—thus underlining the very high quality of his information—but also to show how conservative are the societies we are studying here. Conservative in odd ways, as we shall see. It is, of course, desirable to avoid confusing social forms with their content; and it is quite deplorable to attach importance only to what has lost all meaning. Here, however, we have to note that although human societies may sometimes resemble verterbrates, whose skeletons outlive their envelope of flesh, they may be also sometimes be like molluscs, whose body disappears entirely while only the carapace escapes the destruction of death. 'Social shells'-sometimes re-used by several series of usurping hermit-crabs—and then broken, fragmented, and scattered into almost indestructable debris: that is what we call folklore. But to say 'folklore' is to say 'historical population': for among peoples with no known past it is hard to distinguish, in any coherent system we may one fine day perceive, what may have been borrowed from predecessors. Things are otherwise in the Mediterranean basin. There we can find a large number of *present-day* customs whose immense antiquity we find attested since the dawn of writing, or even a little

---

42. They are to be found in ancient authors like Pomponius Mela, who may have drawn their information either from the book itself, or from the oral tradition that sprang from it.

earlier: like that abhorrence of the pig which may legitimately be deduced from the neolithic excavations of Middle Egypt.[43]

Evergreen Foliage and Deciduous Roots

Great changes, of course, have supervened—in the world in general and the Maghreb in particular—during the twenty-five centuries that separate us from Herodotus's description. Seeking to relate the twenty peoples he enumerates to contemporary groupings is thus an arduous undertaking today. Ibn Khaldun is much nearer to us, yet we still get lost trying to track down present-day tribes on the checker-board he presents. Let us rather imagine the ancient civilizations of the Maghreb like necklaces: from time to time a thread breaks and the beads roll from shore to shore and intermingle, then the thread of a new State reunifies them all in a different order; the beads are still the same, but it is no longer the same necklace.[44]

The earliest ethnographer of the Maghreb happened to take an interest in the structures of kinship—in other words, in what is most essential, most fundamental in a society. For the achievements of civilization are easily borrowed, as we can see daily, but when a society changes its structures, that is an event so momentous it cannot be explained otherwise than by some internal maturation. The Maghreb—where transient things (like female fashions, hair styles, or 'correspondents' reports') were apparently immutable, from prehistory to our own times; where the most notoriously Islamic (and hence imported at a particular historical date) 'achievements of civilization' were nonetheless already established a thousand years before the preaching of the Koran—is now about to reveal its roots to us: roots so different from any we

---

43. See note 18 above.
44. The same observation—this time applied to anthropological types rather than to artefacts—was made as early as 1886 by M. Collignon (*Bulletin de Géographie Historique*, p. 282): 'It may be said that there is no locality where it is not possible to find several, if not all, of the types scattered across the territory.' What he says of Tunisia is more or less true throughout the Maghreb; each region is, however, characterized by a particular blend of types.

might uncover today! Strange plant, with evergreen foliage and deciduous roots!

Uncertain Jealousy

Let us now let the witness speak, simply taking note of everything in his account, without exception, that directly concerns our subject. He will name, locate, and briefly describe some twenty peoples; but some of these have the same customs as their neighbours, so that he gives us only five social patterns.

First people (starting from Egypt). 'Their women wear a bronze ring on each leg, and grow their hair long...[they take] girls who are about to be married to see the king. Any girl who catches his fancy, leaves him a maid no longer.'[45] *Sixth people.* 'Each of them has a number of wives, which they use in common, like the Massagetae— when a man wants to lie with a woman, he puts up a pole to indicate his intention. It is the custom, at a man's first marriage, to give a party, at which the bride is enjoyed by each of the guests in turn; they take her one after another, and then give her a present—something or other they have brought with them from home.'[46] *Tenth people.* 'Next come the Gindanes. The women of this tribe wear leather bands round their ankles, which are supposed to indicate the number of their lovers: each woman puts on one band for every man she has gone to bed with, so that whoever has the greatest number enjoys the greatest reputation for success in love.'[47] *Twelfth and thirteenth peoples.* The Machlyes and the Auses have similar customs, to wit: 'They hold an annual festival in honour of Athene, at which the girls divide themselves into two groups and fight each other with stones and sticks;[48] they say this rite had come down to them from time immemorial, and by its performance they pay honour to their native deity—which is the same as our Greek Athene. If any girl, during the course of the battle, is fatally injured and dies, they say it is a proof that she is no

---

45. The Adyrmachidae. *Histories*, Book Four, 168.
46. The Nasomenes. *Histories*, Book Four, 174.
47. The Gindanes. *Histories*, Book Four, 176.
48. The description of this game exactly corresponds to the Kora (see note 27 above), a ritual game of the present-day Maghreb.

maiden. Before setting them to fight, they pick out the best-looking girl and dress her up publicly in a full suit of Greek armour and a Corinthian helmet; then they put her in a chariot and drive her round the lagoon.' Regarding their marriage customs: 'The women of the tribe are common property; there are no married couples living together...When a child is fully grown, the men hold a meeting, and it is considered to belong to the one it most closely resembles.'[49] *Nineteenth people* '...the Zaueces: amongst this people the drivers of the war-chariots are the women'.[50]

Herodotus gives us no further information on the family structures of North African forbears. Despite their brevity, however, these few notes at least steer us away from explaining the (undeniable) conjugal jealousy of the Maghreb's present-day inhabitants by heredity. On all other points, by contrast, they underline the extreme social conservatism of the region's non-urban areas. So far as one can tell, jealousy is a natural feeling. It may in fact be encountered, in varying degrees and circumstances, on all continents. On its own, therefore, the existence of jealousy does not betray the influence of society. On the other hand, the total absence of jealousy in a situation in which it would normally be observed, or equally, a generalized excess of it, are social facts. Well, the former state of affairs is described as having prevailed among a certain population, while the latter (opposite) case is precisely what we encounter among that same population in our own day. To explain this curious substitution, we must now analyse the fraternal relationship: first between two brothers, then between brother and sister.

49. The Machlyes and Auses. *Histories*, Book Four, 180.
50. The Zaueces. *Histories*, Book Four, 195.

5

'Lo, Our Wedding-Feast Is Come, O my Brother'[1]

Whether descent is patrilineal or matrilineal,[2] we find that one bond always remains fundamental in the old societies of the Maghreb: that of brotherhood. This brotherly bond is so universally decisive that we may quite safely complete the first ethnographer's text and assert that the group of husbands who used to share a group of women was not assembled by cooptation, election, or chance, but was united by a pre-existing and indestructible bond: brotherhood. The 'co-husbands' of whom Herodotus speaks were men from the same *ferqa*, or rather from an almost identical group which obviously bore a different name.[3] As for women, the implication of this history for them (in a distant past, of course) is some degree of confusion between the relationships of wife and sister-in-law.

In the present, and throughout the known past everywhere in the Maghreb, we find this brotherly bond associated with a maximum of privileges and duties. Two men born of the same father (north of the Sahara) or of the same mother (south of the Sahara) have more than just the same name: they have the same honour and the same 'personality'. In matters of vengeance, they are strictly interchangeable; and I have known many (contemporary) instances in

---

1. The singer is a bride, and the original text has 'thy wedding-feast' ('with me' being implicit). To convey the real meaning in another language, this has to be translated 'our wedding-feast'.
2. Both systems exist among the Berbers, but the second is no longer encountered except among the Tuareg, and not all of them, at least nowadays.
3. On the *ferqa* (clan), see pp. 118–19 below.

which men expected to die for the crime of one of their brothers.[4] Yet this sharing of every kind of benefit or disappointment, which characterizes the relationship between brothers in the Maghreb, does not at all imply familiarity. The eldest brother is almost as highly respected as a father: one must lower one's eyes in his presence; not smoke in front of him; move away if he is in the company of other men, to avoid any risk of hearing a joke that—if his younger brother were there—would cause him to blush. In many Maghreb families, younger brothers call the eldest *sidi* (my lord); and conversely the eldest brother, before he even reaches adolescence, acquires the habit of laying down the law to his younger brothers and sisters.

My Lord Brother

The youngster is indeed destined for great responsibilities. For if the family property remains undivided—a situation of which I have known many instances, especially in the Aurès before 1940—he will have the honour and duty of managing the entire common patrimony. This is another point on which the facts of History do not seem to match those of ethnography. The historian (while noting an optional, or more or less moral, privilege of the eldest son) points to the equality that prevails among sons in the Middle East, Greece, India, and China, which is reflected in division of the patrimony.[5] Attributing this rule of inheritance exclusively to the despotic state, he thus contrasts it with that which prevailed in Medieval Europe, where one manifestation of freedom was the first-born's privilege in matters of inheritance. Yet it is precisely in those regions where we have evidence of an equal sharing of inheritance among sons going back to early antiquity[6] (Greece, Babylonia, Egypt) that we find the highest respect for the first-born;

---

4. See pp.121 ff. below.
5. Karl A. Wittfogel, *Oriental Despotism*, New Haven 1957, p. 79.
6. Very long before Islam, at any rate. As is well known, the latter prescribes equal division among sons, and for each daughter a portion equivalent to half a son's portion. This division among sons was not an innovation in the Middle East, but the participation of the daughters, mother, and widow in the inheritance was.

while in countries in which the latter's privilege in matters of inheritance still operates (England), or did so until recently (France), brotherly relations are fairly egalitarian.

In reality, the contrast between the circumstances we may observe today and those whose distant traces may be discerned in history is less great than it seems. For in Pharaonic Egypt: 'the eldest son, who had important ceremonial tasks, received a larger share of his father's estate. But the remaining children also could claim a legally prescribed share of the total. The principle of more or less even division is clearly stated in the Babylonian code. A present made by a father during his lifetime to the first-born is not included in the final settlement .... Assyrian law is more complicated. Again the eldest son has an advantage, but all other brothers are entitled to their share. In India the eldest son's originally privileged position was gradually reduced.'[7]

'Don't Cry, Chapelon'

As everyone knows, in France primogeniture was officially abolished by the French Revolution. But in numerous families it actually survived up to the beginning of the twentieth century (in my mother's family, for instance, which came originally from the Massif Central). Nowadays, children are treated identically almost everywhere. There are a few exceptions, however, all in the south, and most on the left bank of the Rhône between the Ventoux and the sea.[8] There, in old families, people over fifty still call younger sons by their given names, using the surname for the eldest and for him alone. In certain of these same families, the eldest has been addressed from birth with the formal *vous*, while the familiar *tu* has always been used with all the other children. A little scene, a slice of life thirty years ago, in a Lyons tram: a matron, trying to comfort her three-year-old offspring, who was bawling with all his might, told him: 'Don't cry, Chapelon [the child's surname], I'll buy you a carp with a nice egg sack you can pop.' Chapelon calmed down,

---

7. Wittfogel, pp. 79–80.
8. Much more isolated cases are still to be found on the borders of Lozère and Haute-Loire.

while the ethnographer noted that the little tyrant was the eldest son of a French family from the south-east.

South of the Mediterranean, the situation is exactly the opposite, for among brothers there we find at once a very ancient tradition of equality in matters of inheritance and a real inequality to this day in family protocol. An intelligent little boy from the Middle Atlas once told me: 'I'm my father's eldest son. That seems to be very important.' Among present-day Tuareg, a brother's rank is still so basic that, in practice, a Tuareg will use the word that literally means 'brother' (son of my mother: *aïtma*) only to denote in a general way all his relatives.[9] For his true brothers, he will say 'my elder brother' (*amaqqar*) or 'my younger brother' (*amadray*). Even for a male or female parallel cousin, he will use these words; and a man will say of a girl, who may perhaps be younger than him, she's my *tamaqqart* (literally, 'my old woman'): this then means that she is his first cousin, the daughter of his father's elder brother or of his mother's elder sister. In this same region, inheritance faithfully follows Koranic law—one share to each daughter, two to each son—but rights can be transmitted only by daughters (at least in the Ahaggar), and sovereign rights first to the eldest son of the eldest maternal aunt or the eldest sister.

The right of primogeniture, like many other privileges, can also become a burden. I know many young Algerians who owe their higher education to the arduous factory labour of an illiterate elder brother who was their true father. In Morocco, an elder brother of good family will hesitate to marry before having settled his sisters. In Lebanon, a parentless girl will not dare do so without authorization from her elder brother, even if she is legally of age. In Greece (Argolis), young Nikos was almost thirty in 1964, but his first concern was to marry off his sister and get his younger brother an education, and only then to start a family himself.

Throughout the Old World, then, both north and south of the Mediterranean, the modern observer can collect distinctive ancient customs that nevertheless resemble one another. Almost every-

---

9. To define kinship more precisely, nowadays people say: *aïtma win ti*, literally 'sons of mothers, my father's ones', for relatives on the father's side; *aïtma win anna*, 'sons of mothers, my mother's ones', for relatives on the mother's side.

where, men can thus be encountered whose position within their families—as first-born—was quite risky from a psychological point of view. This young fellow—whom his younger brothers treat as an important person; whom his father (out of modesty) does not dare kiss in front of an adult member of the family;[10] who is fawned upon by his mother, grandmother, aunts, and sisters—may easily become unbearable unless he is remarkably good-natured. A proverb picked up in Tlemcen says: 'The Muslim household is made up of the king, the queen, the pig, and the beast of burden'. The king is the baby, the last-born or m'azouz (aftercrop); the queen is the mother;[11] the beast of burden is the father of the family. As for the pig, that is the elder brother.

To sum up, respect for the first-born is a feature common to the entire Ancient World, whether among sedentary agriculturists, nomads or town-dwellers, in a region where kinship follows the male line or in one of the residual matrilineal areas. Equal division of the inheritance among sons often coexists with an almost filial respect for the elder brother, and an almost paternal devotion on the latter's part. It is very possible, if not probable, that equal division of the inheritance is older than the Islam that prescribes it, at least in the Maghreb. There, it was certainly not the result of intervention by a despotic state (as has been claimed to be the case in the Levant[12]). It is easily explicable nowadays by the fact that it 'coincides' with Koranic law, which may seem sufficient explanation. But in fact the explanation is not sufficient: after all, with respect to female inheritance peasant Maghreb has blithely dispensed with obedience to Islam. If it has been entirely obedient so far as male inheritance is concerned, that is because the latter apparently was not inconvenient, or perhaps already conformed to its practice.

It seems to me, in fact, that in the old Maghreb, as in republican Greece, the *tawsit*, the *ferqa*, the clan, the tribe—whatever name is given to the group—had even greater need of men than of land or

---

10. Especially his father-in-law (wife's father), his own father, and his elder brother (the latter to a lesser extent).
11. In Tlemcen, the wife is a cousin, closely secluded but respected and rarely repudiated.
12. According to Wittfogel, p. 84.

sheep. For what use is a patrimony that is not defended? When individual ownership became generalized, equal division may then have had the function of retaining younger brothers. This need for men could be combined, moreover, with a traditional structure of command that for its part still privileged the first-born son. In rural areas, indeed, until quite recently, the common patrimony was still more managed than owned, and this management was carried out by the Elder: the oldest surviving male of the oldest generation.

The Honour of Sisters

Throughout the Mediterranean area, north and south, the virginity of girls is a matter that, oddly enough, concerns primarily their brothers, and their eldest brother most of all. A little male child of seven is thus already trained to act as chaperon to a ravishing adolescent girl, in full knowledge of exactly what kind of peril she is exposed to. This danger is presented to the child as a cause of the most terrible shame, which cannot fail to cast an entire proud family into abjection, besmirching even the glorious ancestors in their graves. And he, snotty kid that he is, is held personally accountable to his family for the so intimate little capital of the beautiful girl who is part servant to him and part mother, the object of his love, tyranny, and jealousy alike—in a word, his sister.

It is not at all astonishing that *throughout the Mediterranean* such 'conditioning' of the little man leads to a given number of stereotyped crimes. Here is one, taken at random, whose victim was a young Italian poetess, contemporary with François I—but this sort of crime is still current in Greece, Lebanon, Iraq,[13] and throughout the Maghreb. Isabella Morra, daughter of the baron of Favale, was born in 1521 and murdered at the age of twenty-five.[14] 'In the nearby castle of Bollita (today Nova Siri), there lived a Spanish nobleman, Don Diego Sandoval de Castro, the Governor

---

13. In 1964, the press reported two decrees of General Aref, one granting a full pardon to forty-three brothers who had killed their sisters; the other reducing to one year all sentences of longer duration meted out for 'crimes of honour'.

14. Dominique Fernandez (*The Mother Sea*, London 1967, p. 56) tells her story, following the Italian scholar Benedetto Croce. Three songs and ten sonnets by her are known.

of Cosenza, who was also a poet. Most probably there was never any exchange between Isabella and Don Diego but that of verses. The two young people probably never met. *But*, one day when Don Diego had sent her a letter (or more poems: it is not clear which) by the intermediary of the Morras' tutor, Isabella's brothers intercepted the missive, murdered the messenger, stabbed their sister, and, still not satisfied, killed the Spanish nobleman in an ambush.' Regarding this exemplary old crime, Dominique Fernandez mentions 'the masculine ferocity guarding the sister's virtue' and 'the "crime of honour", or incestuous jealousy disguised as family defence.'

To avoid weighing this study down, I am limiting quotations and references. But here is an author in the public domain— Stendhal— and a 'Christian' story that took place four centuries ago (in 1559, to be precise): 'On the 30th, Don Leonardo del Cardine, the Duke's kinsman, and Don Ferrante, Conte d'Aliffe, the Duchess's brother, arrived at Gallese and entered the Duchess's apartments to take her life.'[15] One of the priests (present to give the duchess extreme unction) commented to her brother that it would be as well to wait until she had given birth before killing her. The brother replied: 'You know that I have to go to Rome, and I do not wish to appear there with this mask on my face.' Further on, Stendhal comments: 'A few years later, Prince Orsini married the sister of the Grand Duke of Tuscany; he suspected her of infidelity and had her poisoned in Tuscany itself, with the consent of the Grand Duke her brother,[16] and yet this was never imputed to him as a crime. Several Princesses of the House of Medici died in this way.'[17] Stendhal attributes these customs to 'Italian passion'. What passion? For we are not dealing with a husband's jealousy: it is the brother who kills his own sister.

---

15. Marie-Henri Beyle (de Stendhal), *The Abbess of Castro and Other Tales*, London 1926, p. 230.

16. Stories of this kind are told in the villages of Morocco and Kabylia, but not in the Aurès, where a woman is sometimes killed by her husband but never by her father or brothers. (As is well known, the Koran forbids the slaying of an adulterous wife when only indirect proof exists. It requires the adultery to have been *seen* by several witnesses. The Gospels forbid it outright.) Mediterranean Christians and Muslims are at one in paying no heed to these prohibitions or restrictions.

17. Stendhal, pp. 232–33.

The little tyrant, the young paterfamilias, is usually also an individual who has been frustrated. Indeed, in the Maghreb, the mother belongs to the last-born: she is at his disposal day and night, while he is her sovereign, sole, unchallenged master. During the day, the child remains glued to her, moving about on her back or dozing at her knee; at night he sleeps naked against her, skin to skin. He suckles when he wants, sleeps, wakes, and evacuates at will. Behind the mother, in a benevolent haze, familiar beings move about— sisters, aunts, grandmothers, fathers, uncles— the child has difficulty distinguishing between them. They all caress him as they pass and hardly ever gainsay him.

When a new birth occurs, within a few hours he loses everything: his place in the bed and at the breast, the total, unforgettable mastery over another being. The emotional shock is always intense, so much so that severe illnesses sometime result—frequently enough for nostrums to exist whose function is to ward them off from the child. In Oranie, for example, to prevent the penultimate child from hating the newcomer and falling ill or dying from this hatred, an egg is prepared for him—a favourite delicacy. But first it is placed between the baby's thighs until he soils it. This operation is undoubtedly magic in character. The jealous child can also cast a spell on the newborn infant: 'eat' him, as the popular saying goes. The illness seems to be known throughout Algeria, with similar symptoms, but it does not have a name everywhere. In the Bône region,[18] it does have a name: *bou-ba'ran,*[19] which refers to its principal symptom—*ba'ran* means anus, and jealousy causes the anus to protrude. As an antidote, seven dates are dipped in blood from the delivery and given to the frustrated child to eat; at the same time, the whole family redoubles its tender attentions towards him. Throughout Algeria, it is customarily said to a man who detests another: 'Yet he wasn't born after you.'

The birth of a brother is not the sole crisis of childhood. As soon as the male child is old enough to understand, in many families he

---

18. Claude and Mabrouka Breteau have studied 'social illnesses' in the Bône region; part of their documentation appears in the unpublished paper by Claude Breteau (École Pratique des Hautes Études, sixth Section), deposited on 1 March 1964 and entitled 'Nord-Est Constantinois, premier palier de la personnalité'.
19. This name is used in Algiers.

will feel great anxiety concerning his mother's precarious situation in the home, for a paternal whim is sufficient to deprive her of it. And the child knows this very early on. During the years I spent with the semi-nomads of the southern Aurès, I often received adult confidences in which the memory of this childhood anguish figures; and I saw a little boy of thirteen weep as he told me: 'If my mother is sent away, I shall commit suicide.' (This happened in 1935, and there had never been any suicide in the Aurès up to that date;[20] but the kid had been to school and knew the word.)

I have spoken briefly of the child's relations with his father and eldest brother: distant, respectful, awkward relations, which are established as soon as he leaves the wet nurses' skirts. It is necessary also to mention his possessive love for his mother, and the fact that very early on the little boy becomes the guardian responsible for his sisters. We have seen how, north and south of the Mediterranean alike, a kid of under ten will quite normally accompany the daughters of the family as a bodyguard and chaperon; and this type of sibling relationship may evolve into an immense mutual tenderness or a hateful despotism.[21]

It is not, however, my intention here to study the traumas suffered by children in the Maghreb during the first years of their lives. I only wish to point out that this childhood terrain is as propitious as any other for the precocious torments that form and deform the spirit. It is a fact, at all events, that on both shores of the Mediterranean, supposed 'crimes of passion' are proportionately more numerous than elsewhere in the world; and it is also a fact that among the causes favouring them, the dramatic background of childhood cannot be excluded.

Manufacturing Jealousy

This, however, is not the most decisive factor. We shall probably get closer to the truth if we reverse the usual explanations: it is not jealousy that most frequently inspires crime, but crime (or its social

---

20. Suicide was very rare in Algeria before 1940, though a few cases were cited in the towns, especially Constantine. Nowadays it is common.
21. In North Africa, a widowed or divorced sister normally comes to live in her brother's household, where she often enjoys more authority than his wife.

image) that manufactures jealousy. In fact, in southern Europe and northern Africa a real scenario of female infidelity exists, which all inhabitants of these regions know by heart from the tenderest age. When conditions favouring tragedy arise within a family, by degrees the whole social machinery creaks into motion, mustering its powerful forces to oblige each actor to conform to the role that has been assigned him since earliest antiquity. In the tribes among which I lived in the Aurès, I had an opportunity to get to know quite well people and families who had figured in crimes of this kind, which even magistrates call crimes of passion. This is how I came to realize that murderers could be literally *coerced* into murder by their relatives, virtually kicked into it, one might say. In the case of one man (who was my cook for a time after his crime), his paternal uncles had made public death-threats in order to force him to kill his wife's putative lover. They had succeeded. Yet the poor killer had openly sympathized with his rival and detested his wife of whom he had been only too anxious to rid himself.

Of course, real, violent feelings may reinforce the effects of conformism and fear of what others may think; but as we have just seen, such feelings are not indispensable. In fact, far more often than one might expect, weakness, docility and malleability are enough to provide the ration of blood and the memorable tales so harshly exacted by public opinion. So public opinion is the real culprit. But what is this public opinion? Whence comes this cannibalistic need of Mediterranean society? How has the most anciently civilized society in the world managed to fashion this deepset mould, which from generation to generation it presses against men's malleability? Of course, in North Africa as elsewhere, megalomaniac tyrants exist, and sufferers from anxious jealousy may also be encountered. But multiple social causes foster these two character traits, and above all the exaggerated value attached to virility, which thus becomes a cause of extreme anguish for the man, perpetually obliged to compare himself with an 'ideal' model of the perfect braggart. In addition, early childhood here is characterized by frustrations just as cruel as those to which middle-class youngsters are subjected in the 'sanitized' civilization of northern Europe and America.

I recommend that readers of this chapter see, or see again, two excellent ethnographical films—*Divorce, Italian Style* and *Seduced and Abandoned*—whose author, Pietro Germi, is undoubtedly a moralist and remarkable sociologist. Their plots, full of humour but basically sinister, are typically Italian. Yet I have known Algerian women who wept when they saw them in Paris, so powerfully did the hateful atmosphere of some passages remind them of the terrors of their own childhood. Through a series of scenes that constitute a real caricatural anthology of Mediterranean society, we see sexual obsession imposed on men, not just by total separation of the sexes, but also by a sort of etiquette that obliges any boy to pay court to any woman he may find himself alone with. We may also note the kind of silent, universal acceptance that surrounds prostitution.[22]

The boy—but especially the eldest son—is an idle kind on whom the servile attentions of all the women in the family (from six to eighty) converge. In return for which he must always be a kind of Cid Campeador, ever ready to butcher all men and violate all women. On occasion this sort of latent aptitude ever required of him must cease to be merely implicit, and the poor Rodríguez is warned that he is going to have to 'show what he can do'. Pending the demonstration, social pressure steadily mounts until it becomes intolerable: first it comes from the family, then the whole town joins in. No shilly-shallying either, since there is only one solution: to kill. Throughout the Mediterranean, confronted by any incident, society, previously congealed in obscure quarrels, automatically divides into two camps: supporters and enemies. Until vengeance has been satisfied, your supporters will hug the walls, their heads bowed in shame beneath the mockery of your enemies. Then that tiny gesture that is expected of you—a finger squeezing a trigger—will reverse the positions of the two sides. And you will have accomplished what you were brought into the world for.

Women, Like Fields, Are Part of the Patrimony

To understand this imposed jealousy, we must now investigate the forms taken by tribal endogamy (or what is left of it) all round the

---

22. It is not limited to Sicily. A Provençal doctor, who knew his village well, told me that a majority of married men regularly frequented the brothel there, with their wives' full knowledge (October 1965).

Mediterranean. *Almost* all the old Maghreb is decidedly endogamous. But that proves nothing about its very distant past,
since a few rare traces of another structure can also be encountered
there, and shifts are taking place before our eyes in these seemingly
immobile areas.[23] Other, more valid reasons militate in favour of a
relative antiquity of endogamy: mainly its diffusion. For it is not
just Arab, or just Berber, but belongs to the oldest Berber 'personality' and to the oldest Arab 'personality', with a high probability that there was no borrowing by one from the other. As we
have seen, its domain may also be extended beyond the Arab-
Berber universe, to the Semitic area as a whole, and even further, to
the entire Ancient World. But let us begin our rapid overview with
the probable epicentre of the phenomenon: the Mediterranean
Levant.

Jacques Berque, speaking of Iraq, writes: 'Another custom,
which belongs to a common stock of institutions already recogniz-
able in pre-Islamic days, has spread beyond the bedouin world,
since it even constitutes a sign of aristocracy in city society. This is
what is known as "preferential" marriage, which entitles the son of
the paternal uncle...to claim the hand of his cousin. This agnatic
trend is so strongly marked among the Ahwâr that the *mahr*[24] is
duly scaled down in accordance with the parental proximity of the
suitor, while the uncle has a right of veto....over his niece's marriage and the right to impose penalties if this is disregarded.'[25]

In Syria and Lebanon I have found numerous examples of marriages between first cousins in the father's line. This practice has
likewise remained very much alive in Iran, among Muslim tribes
like the Bakhtiars and Kashgais, and of course still more in minority groups. Druzes have told me of it in their own families, and in
societies of Zoroastrian origin the practice is even more pronounc-
ed, for the Zoroastrian holy marriage was celebrated between an
uncle and his niece, an aunt and her nephew, or even a mother and
her son or a father and his daughter. Today, strict endogamy sur-

---

23. For example, not long ago (less than three centuries) Tuareg society embarked on a revolution: it shifted from matrilineal to patrilineal descent.
24. Marriage-portion.
25. Jacques Berque, *The Arabs*, London 1964, p. 173.

vives in those Persian milieux that were Zoroastrian, and marriages take place only between first cousins.[26]

Among Christians in the Orient (a minority in Asia Minor, as Jews were everywhere), the clergy favours marriages between a niece and her father's brother to this day. Such unions require a dispensation, but in the regions of the Orient where Christians are a small minority, this is never refused.[27] This favour is due, I have been told, to fear lest the Melchite population, once getting used to marrying non-relatives, might subsequently take this mingling further and accept unions with Muslims, Jews, or Orthodox Christians. Given its small numbers, this might help to pare it down, for mixed marriages ultimately benefit the more populous community, and small minorities shun them.

To be sure, economic motives sometimes help to reinforce tradition: consanguineous marriages are favoured to avoid excessive sub-division of family holdings. Such considerations, however, are insufficient to explain the frequency and persistence of these survivals. For very often the family holding is almost non-existent, and there is nothing to divide. That is not, of course, the case described in a book devoted to the Rothschild family: '...on 11 July 1824, [Mayer's youngest son] James walked under the *chupa* (the Jewish wedding canopy) with Betty, his own niece, child of his brother Salomon. It quickly became a dynastic dogma that, as in the case of the Habsburgs, the most brilliant possible match for one member of The Family was another.[28] Out of the twelve marriages consummated by the sons of the original five brothers, no less than nine were with their uncles' daughters. Of fifty-eight weddings contracted by the descendants of old Mayer, exactly half took place between first cousins.'[29] It is, however, very likely that pure tradi-

---

26. I am indebted for this information to Mme Perrier, art photographer, who lived among them for a time. As can be seen, legal 'incest' in the Ancient World was by no means confined to Pharaonic Egypt.

27. Particularly in Lebanon, the dispensation is never refused. In modern Greece, by contrast, the Orthodox Church has taken up a rigid position against marriage between cousins, and has virtually succeeded in suppressing it (see p.00).

28. In fact, it was an extremely ancient tradition, as the Old Testament copiously testifies (see the section of chapter 3 above entitled 'Patriarchs of Israel').

29. Frederic Morton, *The Rothschilds. A Family Portrait,* London 1962, pp. 59–60.

tion, religious considerations, and the particularism characteristic
of minorities played a far more important role—even among the
nineteenth-century Rothschilds—than the cult of the Golden Calf.
On this point, there is a great difference nowadays between the
north-east and the south-east of the Mediterranean. We have seen
how tolerant the Christian clergy in Lebanon is with respect to endogamous marriages, blessing even the marriage of an uncle with
his own niece. In Greece, by contrast, the Orthodox Church forbids
it absolutely: 'It is a marriage of the Devil', a young Greek woman
told me. The Church refuses to bless marriages not just between
first cousins, but also between second and third cousins—in other
words, to the eighth degree.[30] In-law relationships are also a bar to
marriage there; but this barrier extends only to the fourth degree.
At all events, these prohibitions mean that two brothers cannot
marry two sisters, and that a brother and sister cannot marry into
the same family (a form of marriage forbidden by the Koran, but
still common in Kabylia and other Muslim areas). They also mean
that the bonds of kinship have a tendency to extend much further
than in the rest of the Mediterranean.[31]

'Our Son's A-marryin' a Furrin Girl!'

The Catholic clergy in France has been openly combating family
endogamy for centuries, in particular by requiring dispensations
for marriages between close relatives. Certain superstitions and
vague eugenic concerns similarly act as brakes. Yet a quite pro-
nounced family endogamy survived up to the Second World War,
though the forms of opposition just enumerated perhaps explain
why it remained very discreet and was not made famous by picturesque customs. For we must be careful not to entirely confuse
family endogamy with territorial endogamy, which is much more
spectacular, and reported by all folklorists in all our provinces:
'...the importance of this tendency in French social usage is still

---

30. There is no civil marriage in Greece. (It was introduced by the Papandreou
government in late 1982—*Translator's note*.)
31. They also mean that an ethnographical study of the history of marriage in
Greece would be extremely interesting (it should never be forgotten, moreover, that
this is the homeland of the 'Oedipus Complex').

symbolically attested by a number of marriage customs, notably
that of the barrier or barricade...by means of which the young people of the village pretend to oppose a local girl's marriage with a
"foreigner"—who may sometimes live only a few kilometres away,
or even in a neighbouring parish.'[32]
In a very recent past, the opposition was not merely symbolic.
Quoting Abbé Georges Rocal, Arnold van Gennep stresses that
what he says of Périgord is valid for all other regions.[33] 'Formerly,
only people of the same village danced together. The girls were not
allowed to be courted by boys from the neighbouring parishes.
Quarrels used to break out at village assemblies when this rule was
relaxed. The day's carousing made the blows exchanged terrible. In
warlike districts, certain forms of vengeance are still wreaked upon
undesirables, who are beaten up in the street or have a treacherous
steel wire stretched across their path.' In this connection, I well
remember the astonishment of a Parisian household staying in a
village in southern Britanny and arriving unexpectedly in the midst
of a family in tears. Upset and embarrassed, they asked the nature
of the misfortune that had overtaken these poor people: 'Our son's
a-marryin' a furrin girl!' Naturally, they commiserated—lengthily.
Then the moment came to seek some consolation to offer the afflicted family: 'Tell us then, where is she from, this foreign girl?'
Fresh outburst of sobbing: 'She's from Nantes.'

At present, though this is a recent development, the number of
consanguineous marriages is rapidly decreasing in France, as a recent survey covering the thirty-two years from 1926 to 1958 shows:
'In the initial period, it can be seen that the coefficient is highest in
the island of Corsica, mountain areas, and rural departments without large urban centres.'[34] In 1926, the lowest average coefficient of
consanguinity occurred in the Gironde (16). The highest were to be
found in Cantal (180), Hautes-Alpes (181), Aveyron (182), Morbihan (188), and finally Corsica (274).

---

32. Arnold van Gennep, *Manuel de folklore français*, Paris 1943, vol. 1, p. 234.

33. Abbé Georges Rocal, *Folklore: le vieux Périgord*, Paris 1927, p. 13 (quoted
by van Gennep, pp. 256–7).

34. Sutter and Goux, 'Évolution de la consanguinité en France', *Population*, 1962,
no. 4, p. 687.

With respect to the last-named department, and in order to show that ethnography is a key that opens many doors—including the comprehension of a figure that Corsican insularity alone is insufficient to explain—we shall content ourselves with quoting the plea for mercy which, in 1760, a young husband from Corte addressed from his prison cell to the authorities holding him (he was guilty of having 'kissed' his wife before marrying her).[35] 'Very Illustrious and Excellent Lord, Angelo Franco Valio, son of Giovanni Bariera, of Corte, humbly submits to Your Excellency that, having fallen in love with Lucie, daughter of the late Baptista Santucci of this place, and his affection having already existed for more than six years, he asked her hand in marriage of Stefano Santucci, her grandfather, and of her nearest relatives, who resolved to give their consent, with the exception of one cousin.[36] The consenting relatives promised to make representation to this cousin to give the writer satisfaction. But, since after some long time they could obtain nothing, they counselled the said Angelo Franco to kiss the girl,[37] thinking that in this wise the desired outcome would be attained. That is what the writer did, with the agreement of the above-mentioned girl. But the above-mentioned cousin swore a complaint regarding the kiss thus given. At once an inquiry was ordered, witnesses heard, and the trial ran its course against the writer. It is for this reason that he very humbly entreats Your Excellency to grant him his mercy, since, in like cases, it has been customary to show compassion, the marriage having besides followed with the consent of all, except the above-said cousin.'

Between 1926 and 1958, the rate of consanguinity in Corsica dropped from 274 to 94; in Cantal from 180 to 37; in Hautes-Alpes from 181 to 30; in Aveyron from 182 to 56; in Morbihan from 188 to 44.

---

35. Quoted by J. Busquet, *Le droit de la vendetta et les Paci Corses*, Paris 1920, pp. 118–9.

36. In connection with this, see the passage on Iraq from Berque's *The Arabs* quoted on p. 104 above.

37. The kiss in question is one of the forms of *attacar*. *Attacar* means 'to attach'. On the *attacar* that might be called a 'strategic kiss', see p. 168 below.

There is not enough space here to quote all the old French songs in which the lover is a cousin. Here is one, at any rate, that I remember:

> How would you have me marry,
> My father won't give me leave.
> My mother still less than my father,
> And (save one) no relative.
> But handsome Jean-Pierre, my cousin...

When Perdican first meets his cousin Camille, whom his uncle wishes him to marry, he greets her with the words 'Good day, dear sister'; subsequently, he loves her but does not marry her, for Musset's heroes do not trifle with love. Baudelaire thus attaches himself to a venerable Indo-European–Semitic tradition when he pens his Invitation to the Voyage: 'My child, my sister...'

Revolutions Come and Go, Mothers-in-law Remain

Among the Muslims of Africa, endogamy is far more evident still; but we do not, as in France, have any statistical survey of the changing rate of consanguinity, so must refer solely to ethnographical 'hearsay' to measure the changes in this domain. Before 1940, I knew some young Algerian intellectuals who were beginning to protest against the obligation to marry a cousin whom the family had chosen for them from birth.[38] A very few were already disobeying their families' wishes. After 1945, considerable numbers had ceased to obey and were marrying as they pleased; now it was the turn of their families to groan.[39] For, over the best-bred girls there still hung the prohibition against marrying otherwise than according to past formulae; unable to marry their 'intended' (who was

---

38. In the more developed towns of the Maghreb, a beginning has been made (out of a concern for eugenics) in formulating warnings against marriages between very close relatives, but only in the last few years.

39. I knew a genuine old Algerian aristocrat, who died very recently, whose last years were painfully afflicted by his disappointment at not having been able to marry off his daughters, in the absence of men of his own rank (i.e. his own blood) to offer them. No misfortune of revolution or war could make him forget this.

having a second shot with some girl from Paris), abandoned maidens had no means of marrying others. Then came the great upheaval of the 1954–62 revolution. Did it accentuate the tendency of young people to free themselves from tradition? It is not yet very clear, for revolutions come and go, while grandmothers and old-maid aunts are everlasting. And since social custom progresses more slowly than politics, it continues to determine a significant number of marriages.

The rule survives with greater strictness in families of high standing. An eldest son of very noble Constantine stock blushed as he quoted to me a saying of his old father's: though very eager to marry off his daughters, the latter nevertheless refused every match and answered his son's urgings with the words: 'One does not allow a blood mare to be covered by a jackass'. The young man who recounted this had immense respect for his father, yet he admitted that on this occasion he had been scandalized by him, and that twice over: first by the form which he found indecent and hardly dared repeat, but also by the content, for he was pained and shocked that his father would make no concession to settle his sisters. Every feeling that can be deduced from this trivial event allows us to situate it at the high point of a revolution. For those girls—strictly brought up in the gynaeceum, capable of running a house and holding their place in it with proud modesty—fiancés had been preordained from the first. But the latter—'great tent cousin's'—after lycée and university had chosen their companions elsewhere. It was already too late to secure the boys' obedience, but still too early for the girls' liberation. Even the vocabulary of the old man, the very reactions (in secret) of his son, locate the anecdote quite precisely in time.

'Lo, Our Wedding Feast Is Come, O My Brother!
Lo, the Day Is Come I Have So Longed For'

Vocabulary always provides valuable pointers to customs of distant origin, and in both Arabic-speaking countries and areas of the Berber language a poet calls the woman he loves 'my sister'. When the author of the love-song is a woman, she calls her lover 'my brother'. In the Aurès, I collected a large number of poems improvised by hired mourners during the funeral vigils that follow a killing (this old custom is still known to be practised from time to time in Corsica).[40] Their strangeness had moved me to note separately four lines composed, after a murder, by the 'widow/cousin' of the dead man. The murder had taken place in 1921 and I recorded this text in 1935, which means that it was considered worth preserving. One further circumstance should be noted. The widow, named Cherifa, was a first cousin of the murdered man, named Hocine; but he had repudiated her a short time before his death, since he was courting a married woman belonging to another *ferqa* of his tribe.[41] He was an only son, and his father had been murdered like him. Hocine was not avenged, and fifteen years later his *anza* still stood on the murdering clan's territory, thus proving that an offense had indeed been committed.[42] For every *ferqa* had its territory, where outsiders could not circulate without being accompanied by a man of the *ferqa*—otherwise they would be suspected (rightly, moreover) of bad intentions.

Here is the text of the song:

Lbalto, djilith
Lbalto, djilith,
Ouma nidji-th,
dhi hqebelith.

Literally:

Overcoat, waistcoat,
Overcoat, waistcoat,

---

40. They unfortunately disappeared (along with most of my notes) during the Second World War.

41. See p. 118 below.

42. After a murder, it was customary in the Aurès to erect a heap of stones on the spot where it had taken place, and it was the murderer's family who carried out this insulting action. The dead man's family, after he had been avenged, came to demolish the pile of stones. I found this custom again in the High and Middle Atlas, but people no longer knew whether it was the dead man's family or the murderer's who put up the monument, and a well-informed old man told me: 'neither one nor the other, but those who want a war'.

> *My brother, we left him*
> *Turned towards the East.*

The words *paletot* (overcoat) and *gilet* (waistcoat), borrowed from French and Berberized, are there to furnish a perfect ryhme for East (*hqebelith*); but also, no doubt, because their strangeness provides food for dreams, evoking the exoticism and luxury 'which Cipango ripens in its distant mines' (José-Maria de Heredia). Our symbolists have no monopoly on affectation.

Twenty-five years later, in September 1962, I picked up this bride's song in the Arabic-speaking Rif. It is the bride who is singing in honour of her future husband:

> *Lo, thy wedding*[43] *is come, O my brother!*
> *Lo, the day is come I have so longed for...*
> *The sons of thy paternal uncles have feasted thee.*
> *And I, what feast shall I make thee?*

The practice of calling a father-in-law 'my paternal uncle' is also encountered almost everywhere in the Maghreb; this is said to be out of politeness, since the word meaning 'paternal uncle' is extremely affectionate and respectful, whereas the word meaning 'father-in-law' is somewhat distant and cold. In the Maghreb, in fact, people call almost everybody *'ammi*: in Lebanon, by contrast, the appellation *'ammi* is reserved for the father-in-law.

The custom whereby a man calls his wife 'cousin' and is called 'cousin' by her in return (even though no kinship exists between the two spouses) is still current usage and very widespread among the Christians of Lebanon; and isolated instances of it may also be encountered in some African Muslim families. The reason then given is 'a married couple's modesty'—but it is also a very delicate, affectionate, and courteous mode of expression. On the opposite shore of the Mediterranean, this usage was observed by my grandfather in 1880 in a small number of families in central and southern France: not without some surprise, since he bothered to recount it

---

43. 'With me' is implicit.

fifty years later, noting that there was no blood relationship between the spouses.

The 'Cousin/Brother' Is a Cousin/Husband

Vocabulary is here a faithful reflection of custom. Apart from some Tuareg and (to a degree) the Moroccan Atlas and the Ouarsenis, throughout the remainder of the great Maghreb—among sedentary agriculturists and transhumants, among nomads and in the old town bourgeoisies—very many people still consider the ideal marriage to be a union between a young virgin and the son of one of her paternal uncles:[44] a first cousin commonly called 'my brother'. The closer the relationship, the more satisfactory the marriage. This aspiration has so formal a character everywhere—in the Oran, Algiers, and Constantine regions, and in the Sahara territories—that I noted that the fact of having exchanged women at any time in the past was considered a presumption of kinship *in the paternal line*.

In the semi-nomadic tribes of the southern Aurès, whose life I shared between 1934 and 1940, current practice then corresponded entirely to the social ideal: marriage between cousins was desired, and marriage between cousins was what actually took place. To tell the truth, it did not correspond to an absolute rule, such as the prohibition against marriage with a foster-sister: theoretically a son might bring in an alien daughter-in-law, and this even happened on occasion without creating any incident. Such cases, however, were rare enough for it to be barely possible, in a group of nearly a thousand souls, to find more than half a dozen women from another tribe. The truth was that this kind of marriage was not really very durable, since the 'foreign woman' would grow bored and leave again. The converse—a woman of the tribe married outside—also existed, and I knew a few instances of it; but it constituted something remarkable and extremely rare. (It should be noted that this

---

44. The cousinship relation among Berbers of the North can be understood better when it has been studied among Berbers of the South: the Tuareg call all parallel cousins (in other words, children whose fathers are brothers or whose mothers are sisters) 'brothers'; they call only *cross*-cousins (children of a maternal uncle or a paternal aunt) *aboubah* (plural: *iboubeh*).

latter type of marriage is disapproved of more strongly than the former, unless it serves to sanction an alliance with a family whose assistance is sought.)

All other marriages took place within the five kinship-groups of a single tribe, and preferably within each kinship-group.[45] I had established their genealogy, with the basic events in the lives of each of the individuals who made them up, going back as far as the oral tradition reached, in other words, to the middle of the eighteenth century (five or six generations). I was thus able to ascertain that this express aspiration of the society had not slackened at any time, though in every period there had been a small number of exceptions. The aspiration was, so to speak, dignified and consecrated by the year's most splendid festival: the marriage that, just before the ploughing, opened the season of nuptials.[46]

For custom required all great weddings (that is to say, marriages of virgin girls) to take place in the course of September, between the short season of fairs and pilgrimages and the October ploughing, and hence immediately after the period in July and August during which, under cover of a religious truce, goods and gossip were exchanged between the North and the South. The moment was doubly favourable, since it corresponded to the brief euphoria following the harvest and these exchanges, and just preceded that union of water and earth which, in early autumn, gives the signal for sowing and ploughing. For 'everything to go well' throughout the year—but first and most crucially the forthcoming harvest—it was necessary that the first marriage, the inaugural marriage, should be the 'best marriage possible'. Two conditions were laid down for this: that the bride and groom should be very close cousins in the paternal line, and that the bride should be a virgin. The reputation, power, and wealth of the two families were also taken into consideration—but secondarily.

During the following years, I knew hundreds of inhabitants of the Maghreb, belonging to every corner of the Arab-Berber subcontinent: all gave me examples of this preference. I recorded it personally in the Aurès, in the two Kabylias, in the Bône region, in

---

45. Between 150 and 300 individuals.
46. This practice can also be found in the Moroccan Atlas.

the Rif, in Mauritania, in part of the Ahaggar, and among the bourgeoisies of Constantine, Bougie, Algiers, Tlemcen, and Tunis. Only the Middle and High Atlas and the Ouarsenis are (to some extent) an exception. Why has endogamy survived so sturdily until our own day, outside its chosen milieu, the nomadic tribe? Several reasons seem to have contributed to this survival, of which the first is easily explained by the desire to combat the parcellization of family holdings imposed on each generation by the Muslim inheritance system. Among minority populations (Eastern Christians, Jews, heterodox Muslims), the will to safeguard a threatened particularism has likewise played a not inconsiderable role. It nevertheless remains the case that these explanations do not explain everything. It is also necessary to take account of both a vigorous tradition and (even in those milieux that have been urbanized longest) a sentimental valorization of endogamous (Bedouin) society.[47] This was not so unjustified, as we shall see in the course of the next chapter.

---

47. Jacques Berque (*French North Africa. The Maghrib Between Two World Wars*, London 1967, p. 195) writes of Tunis: 'How can such family differentiation persist today? through the practice of a kind of endogamy. Not indeed for ritual or religious reasons, nor even out of respect for custom, but simply because the thing is fashionable. For this subtly nuanced way of life is governed by good taste. And in the city, as among the Bedouins, "the uncle's son" has a prior claim to his cousin's hand. This is not the only trait of tribal honour, and thus of Bedouin affinity; we had noted others in connection with a village of the Sahil. Such affinities may perhaps be found throughout the Islamo-Mediterranean world.'

6
Nobility According to Averroës and Nobility According to Ibn Khaldun

Tribal society, still fairly well preserved in certain mountain or desert fastnesses of the Maghreb, has undergone an evolution, or the beginnings of an evolution, everywhere else. Well, it is this evolution, or rather the defensive reactions it has provoked, which I believe to be directly responsible for the debasement of women's condition in the Mediterranean area, in southern Europe as much as in northern Africa and western Asia. This is why the mechanisms that interest us, if we are to understand them, must be analysed at every stage of their evolution, but starting with their point of departure: in other words, beginning with nomadic tribes.

Agriculturists and Nomads

At this stage, it would be normal to broach a classic topic of sociology: the opposition between nomads and settled agriculturists. In the Mediterranean Levant, authors have always described the two societies as fundamentally different. In my view, the analogy with the Maghreb should be more nuanced on this point.

Among Arab-Berbers in the North, hostility often exists between nomads and agriculturists;[1] in the past, the latter were under the former's domination. In the domain of social structures, however, the differences are insignificant. At most, it is possible to discern a greater importance accorded to clan headsmen among nomads; but this is not unknown among sedentary populations. Among the

---

1. Forms of association and contracts between the two types of population may be found.

latter, the importance of the 'council of elders' is predominant; but such councils also exist among nomads. In the matrimonial and family sphere, a whole gamut of transitions from one group to the other can be observed. The same is not true south of the Sahara. There we really find two distinct societies: an apparently homogeneous nomadic society (Tuareg or Moorish) and a sedentary society, dependent upon the former and apparently more heterogeneous. Here is where we should find the greatest analogy with Bedouin society in the Mediterranean Levant.

In addition to these nomadic and sedentary societies, separated by what might be termed a vertical partition since, like a wall, it divides the population into geographical sectors, we may encounter, throughout the Maghreb (north and south alike), more or less distinct traces of a horizontal partitioning, which like a floor cuts society into storeys and, in particular, delimits an intermediary caste between the slave and the free man: the caste of artisans— blacksmiths, butchers, potters, and musicians.[2] The traces of this structure can be found in all the old rural societies of the Maghreb, among Tuareg or Moorish nomads as much as among semi nomads in the Atlas and Aurès or agriculturists in Kabylia.

We may also note that in the Maghreb there are nomads speaking Arabic (the Moors) and nomads speaking Berber (the Tuareg): the former have purely patrilineal descent, whereas in certain districts the latter preserve matriliny.[3] Contrary to what might be supposed, these seemingly fundamental differences have little influence on their respective mores, which are strangely similar, especially insofar as the status of women is concerned.[4]

There is, however, one point that *today*[5] differentiates nomads and agriculturists in the Maghreb: the birth-rate. This difference

---

2. This caste, too, is endogamous, but it is hard to say whether by choice or necessity. It merits a global study, which has not yet been made.
3. Traces of exogamy are found among the latter.
4. See p. 135 below.
5. The nomadic herdsmen described in Genesis reproduced at the same rate as the sedentary agriculturists.

has often been pointed out by geographers and ethnologists.[6] The truth is that from the economic point of view the nomads of today (at least those of the desert zone) represent a society whose productive system is intermediary between hunting/gathering and agriculture. Granted, their livestock may multiply at a rapid rate, but the pastures that provide them with food are renewed at the slow, slow rhythm of nature itself. It is, in fact, just as if the Saharan nomads, thanks to shortage of pastures, had been obliged to preserve rhythms of growth established by palaeolithic hunters—despite the neolithic inventions that ensure a major part of their livelihood.[7]

Celtic 'Clan' and Berber 'Fraction'

Whatever partitioning there may be, we find one fundamental unit appearing throughout the Maghreb under various names,[8] of which the most widespread in Algeria, *ferqa*, is an Arabic word literally meaning 'fraction'. The *ferqa* is indeed effectively a fraction of the tribe. But it is surprising to see this group define itself in relation to the tribe: for the tribe (except in Kabylia) is a fairly loose entity, whereas the *ferqa* is the basic unit of Maghreb society as a whole.

---

6. Edmond Bernus, *Quelques aspects de l'évolution des Touaregs de l'Ouest*, Dakar 1963, p. 28. In the chapter on demography the author notes: 1. among the Tahabanat, one finds 26 unmarried adults (18 men and 8 women) and 16 monogamous couples, which have 28 children altogether; 2. among the Ihayawan, 25 unmarried adults (12 men and 13 women) and 8 monogamous couples which have 9 children altogether; 3. among the Iratafan, 15 unmarried adults (8 men and 7 women) and 6 monogamous couples with fewer than two children apiece. In the Tengueleguedech grouping of Bankilara, out of 40 nobles (*imajeren*), one finds 9 children under 15, 10 adults over 40. Among the 21 adults aged between 15 and 40, there are 15 men and 6 women. Of the 15 men, 8 are unmarried and 4 have no children. Among the Kel Dinnik, the situation is similar.

7. Marceau Gast has collected a very complete documentation on their diet: to this day, it relies heavily on gathering and hunting, which fifty years ago provided most of it. (Marceau Gast, 'Alimentation des populations de l'Ahaggar', *Arts et Métiers Graphiques*, Paris 1968.)

8. The word *ferqa* is used throughout the Arabic-speaking countryside and in numerous Berber districts; in the Aurès, a Berberized form is encountered, *harfiqth* (plural: *hirfiqin*), which the Kabyles pronounce *tharfiqth*. In the same sense, the Tuareg use the word *taousit* (Ahaggar) or *taouchit* (Aïr) in the sense of clan, but also in that of tribe; the word literally means 'palm' (of the hand) or 'sole' (of the foot).

And even in Kabylia, where tribal unity is stronger than anywhere else in the Maghreb, two excellent observers could write: '...remarkable society, in which the village is often dominated by the family and does not interfere with the exorbitant rights of individuals, other than to ensure that they are respected'.[9]

One is at liberty to translate the word *ferqa* by 'clan', provided one makes it quite clear that this term is not being used in the sense given currency by ethnographical literature, but rather in its etymological sense, that which the Celtic word *clanna* possessed at the time of the Roman conquest. Henri Hubert defines the word '*clanna*' as follows: '...it is a Goidelic word which does not designate a type of unit of a definable shape or size. It means "descendant" or "descent". In the plural, for instance, in Irish, *clanna Morna* means the descendants of Morann, but the *clanna Morna* may equally well consitute what sociologists would call a tribe, a family, or perhaps a clan .... So the clan, in the Celtic sense of the word, is something very different from the normal clan, and in particular the totemic clan....The Celtic clans are families, or tribes regarded as families.'[10] The clans of the Maghreb likewise.

Joint Honour

In the Maghreb, the clan appears before us as a reality still immediately perceptible, for it has a frontier, a place in the sun, a name of its own which everyone knows, a collective honour, and even a form of worship: the annual festival of the ancestor, founder of the race. Whether settled or nomadic, it always occupies a particular (vast or confined) territory within which no outsider can claim any right, except for the right to hospitality or to violence. Those who live there are *kin*, residing in a group of tents or houses demonstratively huddled together with all their defences turned outwards. Nothing is more revealing, in this respect, than the physical aspect of the village, encampment, or Arab town house

---

9. Hanoteaux and Letourneux, *La Kabylie et les coutumes kabyles*, Paris 1893, vol. 3, p. 87.
10. *Greatness and Decline of the Celts*, pp. 199–200. He defines the tribe (p. 198) as 'the first self-sufficing social unit'. This is an excellent definition of tribes in the Maghreb.

(whether in the Maghreb or the Levant). Around the house, high windowless walls, jagged with bottle-shards; around the village, all its natural defences, ditches, prickly pears; around the tent, a pack of half-wild dogs, and more terrible even than the dogs, a 'sacralization' of the space that protects it, whose inviolability is identified with honour: *horma.*

In addition to living together, the clansmen share the mysterious bond of blood. This is reflected in the single proper name, which gives the one who has received it at birth an absolute right to the unconditional support of all the others. 'You ask if the Ouled ben Yahya are cousins?[11] Of course, they are cousins. All people from the same *ferqa* are cousins. You say: how can an Ouled Zyane like me be a cousin to the Bellouni, who are Jews,[12] and to the Ouled Aziz and all the others, who are after all Ouled Ahmed? Formerly, when a fellow was worth a lot, the elders of the *ferqa* said to him: be with us like our brother...to strengthen the *ferqa.* And today, because he is from my *ferqa*, he is my brother: he puts his life on the line for me and I do the same for him.'

If one of them is murdered, they will all stand together to avenge him. Conversely, if a man from their group becomes a murderer, they will ruin themselves to help him pay an indemnity called *diya* ('blood price'). In the Aurès before 1940, the *diya* usually stood at 800 douros (4,000 gold francs), though in some cases the tariff could be much higher or much lower. In 1945, one *diya* of 30,000 francs was paid, another of 20,000; in 1935, for four murders committed in the southern Aurès (two on each side), each of the rival families paid the other 100,000 francs. In a land where money is very scarce, these sums are large. It should also be noted that the figure varies with the rate of exchange.[13] The truth is that, within a

---

11. Ouled Ahmed is the Arabic form; my interlocutors in fact would sometimes say *Ah-ahmedh-ou-yahya*, sometimes *ah-hand-ou-yahya*; but all Shawiya know Arabic, whereas few Arabs know Shawiya, so since my aim is not to weary my readers, I have adopted the simplest and most popular way of writing.

12. This should be taken to mean 'who are of Jewish origin' (according to oral tradition), which is the case for quite a number of fractions in Morocco and Algeria. They are actually Muslims.

13. The same is not true of the marriage-portion, which in this region has kept its nominal value irrespective of any ups and downs of the currency.

family of this kind, people are far more than mutually supportive: they are interchangeable. For in the event of a murder, if the *diya* is not accepted by the dead man's family, the latter will take vengeance by killing *any member of the perpetrator's family*. This understandably makes for greater enthusiasm on the relatives' part when it comes to helping a murderer discharge his debt.

'No Man Knows What They Have in Their Hearts'

Among other stories, I recall in 1935 having received a transient visitor in my camp on the Saharan flank of the Ahmar Khaddou, an old man originally from the Ouled-Abderrahman tribe, which was then extending me its kind hospitality. For fifteen years, my casual guest had been living in exile among the neighbouring Ouled Oulèche tribe, thirty kilometres away from his hereditary fields and his house: he did not dare set foot in either of these, because in 1920 his brother had killed a man belonging to another *ferqa* of his tribe. Following this slaying, the murderer's entire family (four households at least, perhaps six) had left the territory. Then, in the course of the next fifteen years, the murderer had died in turn, leaving no children. So fifteen years after the crime and five or six after the death of its perpetrator, the murderer's brother was once again coming to sue for 'pardon'—in other words, permission to pay a very large sum of money to the children of his brother's victim.

The story of this crime is worth analysing, since it encapsulates all the main requirements of Maghreb honour. My visitor's brother was called Si-Mohand-Salah, and he came from a kinship-group adopted by the powerful *ferqa* of the Ouled-Ali-ou-Moussa.[14] One day, he reckoned his honour had been outraged because a man from the Ouled-Khallaf *ferqa*, Ahmed-ou-si-Abderrahman, was courting his wife. To give his revenge the greatest possible éclat, he waited for a great wedding, a propitious occasion, since it is customary to come armed. Furthermore, this particular wedding was taking place in the *ferqa* of the Ouled-Ali-ou-Moussa, among his cousins, which guaranteed him provisional protection. Finally, the

---

14. The kinship group in question was the *Ah' Ahmar-ou-Ahmedh*, adopted as a more or less integral part of the *ferqa* of the Ait-si-Ali-ou-Moussa.

five fractions of the tribe would all be present to see that he was not a man to be insulted with impunity.

The great wedding took place. Si-Mohand-Salah fired at his rival and shot him dead. But the bullet that pierced Ahmed went on to hit one of the wedding-guests Brahim, who belonged to the clan where the feast was taking place, and killed him too. Brahim left no sons, and his father was dead, but he had three brothers. The blood-price was offered to the eldest, Lalmi. He accepted a reduced rate (one thousand francs), because the murderer's family belonged to his *ferqa*, because the murder had been accidental, and because the dead man had no wife or children: all these factors were taken into account and explain the 'knock-down price' Lalmi imposed on Si-Messaoud, the murderer's father. Si-Messaoud and his two brothers (the paternal uncles of the perpetrator and of my old visitor) paid the blood-price jointly, since they all lived in co-parcenary.[15]

The other dead man—Ahmed of the Ouled Khallaf *ferqa*—left behind two small sons: the elder was called Mohand-Salah and the younger, born after his father's death, was given the deceased man's forename. They were brought up, according to custom, by their paternal grandfather, Si-Abderrahman. It was also Si-Abderrahman who was offered the 'blood-price'. He refused it, sending the following reply: 'My son was courting the wife of the man who killed him; he was, therefore, killed rightfully. I take no *diya*. My grandchildren will do as they wish, when they are old enough.'

In 1935, when the perpetrator's brother returned, the two grand-children, now aged eighteen and fifteen, were consulted for the first time. They said: 'We think like our grandfather.' The murderer's brother heard the verdict with consternation, and I saw him set off again with bowed head to the Ouled-Oulèche. For he had an only son and, as the 'Grand Elder'[16] of the injured clan told me pensively a short time afterwards, speaking of his cousins' refusal: 'No man knows what they have in their hearts.' Three years later, in

---

15. They were thus still in the tribe at this time.
16. The eldest brother in the eldest branch of the clan.

1935, Mohand-Salah's brother once again sent a great *jema'a*[17] from the neighbouring tribe with the same request, which was similarly rejected (I was then visiting another valley, so did not meet it). The murderer, his father, his two brothers, and his two uncles—in other words, six households—were all living outside their tribe at the time of my sojourn, between 1934 and 1940. The first four of these households and emigrated solely because of the murder committed by Si-Mohand-Salah; and although it is not as certain that the murderer's two uncles emigrated at the same time,[18] it is very likely, since they helped to pay the first *diya* (the blood-price accepted by a man of their own fraction).

The two great duties of Mediterranean man figure in this story. The first (which recurs in numerous societies) consists in avenging the murder of a close relative. Here, vengeance had not actually been taken, but the threat of it, represented by an old man and two babies, was still enough to cause at least four families, and more probably six, to flee. The other duty was fulfilled, in the most ceremonious fashion, in the presence of the whole tribe: it decrees that the slightest suspicion affecting the virtue of one of the family's womenfolk must be washed out in blood. The fair Helen of this Trojan War was called Barkaoult Mohand. Exceptionally, she and her husband were not cousins, though they belonged to the same tribe. After becoming a widow, she returned to her father in the Ouled-Daoud fraction.

Two Orphans Go to Visit Their Mother

The two orphans, little Mohand-Salah and his younger brother, raised by their paternal grandfather, saw more of their mother's family than other children. This is easily understandable, and presented no difficulty: the two grandfathers lived only three quarters of an hour's walk from each other. Nevertheless, had it

---

17. This word designates the 'senate' of the little republics of the Maghreb, in other words the assembly of family-heads, which takes all decisions concerning the tribe as a whole. The word is also used to denote any meeting of notables.

18. I no longer recall, and most of my documents disappeared in 1942. It can, however, be inferred from the fact that they were still living in coparcenary with the murderer's father at the time of the double murder.

not been for this particular set of circumstances, a little Ouled-Khallaf would not have had the opportunity between 1935 and 1940 assiduously to haunt the territory of a neighbouring but alien *ferqa*. For in these tribes, at that time, though a married woman might move about freely over the territory of her husband's fraction, she did not leave it, even to visit her father, without being accompanied by her husband, her brother-in-law, her son, or one of her brothers, which then became quite a business. But two little orphan boys going to visit their mother—it would be impossible in any country to find that strange.

Their maternal grandfather, and their uncles and male and female cousins on their mother's side, thus grew accustomed to receiving and loving the youngsters. And in October 1939 (when I was still in the country) the elder carried off his mother's first cousin, Fatma-oult-Abdallah. He was then twenty-two and she was about the same age; moreover, she was free, since she had just obtained a divorce, having previously been married off according to custom to a cousin on her father's side, Ahmed-ou-Boumaraf. One had to go back to their great-great-grandfather to find Fatma's and Ahmed-ou-Boumaraf's common ancestor; but since the kinship was on the male side, both belonged to the same fraction, that of the Ouled-Daoud. Fatma did not love Ahmed-ou-Boumaraf, and Ahmed-ou-Boumaraf did not love Fatma; everyone in the tribe knew that Ahmed loved only one woman, named Zohra, who belonged to the *ferqa* of the Ouled-Khallaf and was divorced. No one, however, could marry Zohra, since her first husband, though sanctioning his wife's desertion by repudiating her, had threatened to kill anyone who asked for her in marriage.

Immediately after his enforced marriage with his cousin Fatma, the inconsolable Ahmed-ou-Boumaraf had enlisted, leaving his young wife/cousin in his home. The 1939 war had just begun, and the army then offered the sole escape-route from family tyranny, for in those days no man from this tribe was yet working in France, no one knew so much as a single word of French. In 1939, for an Ouled-Abderrahman of twenty, enlistment was the psychological equivalent of the bottle of Gardenal which a Parisian Bovary gulps down when life no longer holds out any hope.

After her cousin/husband's departure, the abandoned Fatma took refuge with her paternal uncle, Mohand-ou-Belqacem, since her father and paternal grandfather were both dead. Leaving the conjugal home in this way is a frequent occurrence: when a wife is thwarted or neglected by her husband, she will return to her father's house; if he is dead, she will go to her elder brother, or her father's elder brother, or her paternal grandfather. The husband usually waits two or three days, then sends a member of the family as an envoy, with fair words and little gifts. Often the wife returns. If she does not, she is always considered as being divorced. In the event, since Ahmed-ou-Boumaraf had gone off to war, he had not been able to pronounce (in the presence of any witness) the vague formula freeing his cousin, or to state that he did not want Fatma and indeed had not ever wanted her.

Fatma's abduction enraged all the men of the Ouled-Daoud fraction, and in an effort to push the matter to murder they affected to consider that Fatma was not 'truly' divorced. However, before they could have their killing, they had to await the return of Ahmed, the soldier-husband. During this period of cold war between the two fractions, a young bachelor from the Ouled-Daoud fraction, Belqacem, was the victim of a murder attempt. Everyone at once knew that his own cousins had shot at him: 'to warn him'. He had nothing to do with the whole affair, but he was a childhood friend of Mohand-Salah, the young Ouled-Khallaf who had just carried off Fatma, and had not broken with his friend. All the other Ouled-Daoud considered this a crime of high treason, *almost* punishable by death, though not quite: after all, blood is thicker than water.

We may note here that all these complications, which might very easily have become dramatic, would not have occurred if Mohand-Salah's father (the man murdered in 1920 at the beginning of the whole story) had not married a *foreign woman*: in other words, a woman born less than three kilometres from his home, *but into another fraction*.

'Nobility and Honour Can Come Only From Absence of Mingling'

In the fourteenth century, one of the first modern sociologists, the Maghreb's great Ibn Khaldun,[19] speaking of the poorest nomads,

---

19. Ibn Khaldun was born in Tunis in 1332, lived in Granada, Fez, and Tlemcen,

informed his readers: 'Their isolation is...a sure guarantee against the corruption of the blood that results from marriages contracted with outsiders.'[20] Speaking of another, better favoured group: 'Other Arabs living in the hills, where there are fertile pastures and all that makes life agreeable, have allowed the purity of their race to be corrupted by intermarriage with alien families.' Elsewhere the author polemicizes with Averroës, brilliant artisan of a 'Renaissance' that preceded our own by four centuries.[21] Intoxicated by the ancient thought he had helped to revive, and thoroughly imbued with Athenian civic spirit (he was, after all, a town-dweller himself), Averroës had maintained that nobility depends upon a family's antiquity and the number of illustrious individuals it can boast. 'Nobility and honour can come only from absence of mingling', replied Ibn Khaldun two centuries later. And across the abyss of the ages, the oldest Mediterranean aristocracies echo his words (by 'aristocracies' I mean, of course, nomads and peasant proprietors).

So here we have two nobilities. The first—which we may term modern, since it is inconceivable before great cities and states come into existence—was defined by Averroës: it involves studying and comparing the antiquity of lineages and their celebrated scions. In the second, expressed by Ibn Khaldun, there is no study and above all no comparison, for its essence is sustained precisely by the fact

---

and died in Cairo in 1406: in other words, he was the very model of a man of the Maghreb.

20. Ibn Khaldun, *Prolégomènes* [*The Muqaddimah*], vol. 1, (trans. Slane), Paris 1934, p. 272. [Although a modern scholarly English translation of Ibn Khaldun's great work does exist—*The Muqaddimah*, trans. Franz Rosenthal, London 1958—the differences between this text and the French ones cited by Tillion are so considerable that it has seemed best here to retranslate in part from the French passages quoted—*Translator's note.*]

21. Ibid., p. 283 (p. 245 of the Arabic text). Vincent Monteil, on the basis of more authentic manuscripts than those available to Slane, has entirely redone the translation of Ibn Khaldun's work. In this new text, Ibn Khaldun's thought emerges as far richer and more nuanced than in the version we had previously. However, on the precise point of interest to us, the value judgement defended by Ibn Khaldun is not disturbed. In Monteil's translation, I note in particular: '"detribalized town-dwellers" cannot belong to a "house" except in a metaphorical sense...only the clan spirit can create a "house" and a true nobility' ('house' is used here in its royal sense, as in 'house of France', 'house of Austria').

of *standing alone*. Hence keeping one's 'self' intact by preserving it from mixtures, contacts, or confrontations, so sparing it the concealed slight that any comparison, whether defamatory or flattering, implies. Today, south of the Mediterranean, the two nobilities influence each other almost everywhere. Whoever is definitely descended from a particular ancestor held to be glorious is noble, but such certainty exists only in the group that accepts no outsiders. Conversely, the fact of accepting no outsiders is in itself enough to create nobility, and any ancestor then suffices to nurture a sense of pride. And one is always descended from somebody.

Ancestor Worship

In a great number of cases, practice maintains a confusion between the worship of that somebody—an ancestor venerated as such— and the worship reserved (with greater or lesser orthodoxy) for a miracle-working saint or a sharif. This confusion obviously tends to efface the former type of worship, to the advantage of the latter. Yet one may still encounter, precisely in the most isolated and archaic tribes, traditions regarding such and such an eponymous ancestor, who was not a saint, and sometimes even not a Muslim, but whose history nevertheless resembles a hagiographic legend. In addition to the legend surrounding the clan's foundation, we also find its form of worship: that yearly gathering of the ancestor's descendants for a great banquet, which in numerous regions of North Africa is called *zerda*. Do these legends imitate the history of saints, performers of miracles, patrons of towns and clans? The converse seems much more likely, because the lack of orthodoxy of these cults,[22] their exceptionally tenacious roots, and their distribution in my view prove their very great antiquity, Herodotus's testimony in favour of which is merely a supplementary argument.[23]

Despite their archaic nature, these old cults dedicated to an Ancestor (whether holy or secular) at first sight seem less ancient than veneration of the stock itself. In comparison with the latter,

---

22. Maraboutism has long been the bête noire of orthodox Islam.
23. See chapter 4.

they evoke an adaptation, a modernization, and a vulgarization: it is, in fact, easier, and hence more 'common', to be descended from a great and illustrious man than it is (even in the desert) to maintain without admixture a proud line of fierce brigands. Outside the desert, this is simply impossible: for, as Ibn Khaldun rightly observes, the difficulties of the undertaking increase considerably with power and wealth.

Here and there, this kind of 'impossible' and now vanished nobility has, like fossil shellfish, left still finely sculptured imprints. How should we interpret its surviving features, and in particular the desire for endogamy which we have already noted? Are we to suppose that, the more the ancestor's blood has been 'strengthened' in each generation by consanguineous marriages, the nobler his descendants are? Or that they are noble because no (identified) alien blood has come to interrupt, and hence corrupt, the flow issuing from a spring that, while not necessarily glorious or sacred, is authentic and pure. In the former case, the presence of a few drops of a certain blood engenders pride; in the latter, pride is nurtured by an absence: that of the adulteration which any cohabitation entails.[24]

Nowadays, although the Maghreb's nomads and transhumants, like the Kabyles, certainly venerate the blood of the prophet Muhammad, marriage with one of his female descendants is sought only in certain ruling families. Among the nomads and a few very ancient settled peasantries, respect for the race of God's Messenger exists outside any practical matrimonial context; within that context, everyone thinks his own blood is better than anybody else's.

The most ancient nobility consists, essentially, in not 'mingling', hence not frequenting anyone other than kinfolk. It is also noble to receive passing travellers ceremoniously (for three days); to have a touchy sense of honour; to extend effective protection. On this

---

24. Albert de Boucheman, 'Note sur la rivalité de deux tribus moutonnières de Syrie', *Revue des Études Islamiques*, 1934, I. The author records the following attitude among the Arabs of the Levant: 'It is less than honourable not to belong to a great family (and greatness is measured even more by the number of living cousins than by the number of known ancestors)' (p. 18). 'The tendency of the latter [the great nomads] to disdain tribes made up of bits and pieces is in fact well enough known' (p. 27).

slope, however, one must know where to call a halt. For if, convinced as you are that no blood is as good as yours, you attempt to disseminate this view, you will be undertaking a perilous task, in that you will obviously be obliged to maintain relations of some kind with the people you want to persuade. It accurately marks the beginning of decline: the point of transition between ancient caste and modern hierarchies, where one has to elbow one's way forward with—inevitably—greater or lesser distinction.

'The Dunceboroughs Are Part of the Family, That's Why We Receive Them'

North of the Mediterranean, an analogous caste seems to have existed in the distant past, but also almost all trace of it has been effaced. We do know that in our country the Gaulish and Germanic nobilities had already attained the 'Averroës level' well before coming into contact with the first ethnologists: to wit, Tacitus, Pliny, and Caesar. But certain indications make it plausible that an 'Ibn Khaldun' level had preceded the one these authors describe.[25] Subsequently, the various nobilities of the so-called French period underwent the blending we all know about, and then, for centuries, were subjected to the crude catalyses of a tentacular monarchy and to the dictatorship of money. Yet beneath the 'Averroës level', represented nowadays by the descendants of our late lamented court nobility, a different material may be divined, a veritable geological substratum of the former, perpetuated in the fastnesses of a military nobility, impoverished and provincial, in which 'quarterings' are calculated and neighbours ignored.

---

25. Marc Bloch, 'Sur le passé de la noblesse française, quelques jalons de recherches', *Annales d'Histoire Économique et Sociale*, 1936, VIII, p. 367: 'It is not impossible that, in the basic opposition between the seigneurial lords and the countless tenants making up the people, we may be dealing with one of the most ancient lines of cleavage of our civilizations.' Fustel de Coulanges, *Histoire des institutions politiques de l'Ancienne France*, Paris 1924, p. 270: 'The nobility was an institution of old Germany, an institution that intestinal wars had weakened and migrations destroyed. In Roman society, too, there was a nobility. The two nobilities, Roman and Germanic, lasted roughly up to the time of the invasions, and the invasions led to the disappearance of both of them...this German nobility did not resemble the one we have observed in the Roman Empire. It was closer, in fact, to the primitive aristocracy of Ancient Greece and Early Rome.'

Just as I was writing this chapter, I came by chance upon a little book intended for readers knowing only 1,300 words of French.[26] The author describes an old château, where a ten-year-old boy is asking his mother why she receives some tedious elderly cousins: 'The Dunceboroughs are part of the family; that's why we receive them....But it is true that we don't receive many other people at home....Here, it is the family, and the family must be defended against every danger. The unknown is a danger.' This survival is obviously more psychological than real.[27] In other words, it is ideas, prejudices and a folklore which have escaped destruction, rather than lines of descent. But when a coherent set of prejudices has matured in the vast night of prehistory, it terms itself 'feeling' and, beyond any doubt, can survive the shipwreck of institutions for quite a long while.

Golden Age

In a family of this kind (I am now speaking of nomads or semi-nomads in the Maghreb, and no longer of the French provincial nobility), every little country girl I knew was brought up with female cousins on the father's side whom she did not distinguish from her sisters, while her father's sisters and female cousins (who in most cases were identical with her mother's) treated her as their own child. Among the latter was often to be found the mother of her future husband.[28] When the young woman arrived in her new home, a few metres away from the one in which she had been born not many years before, she would continue the relations of intimacy and trust with her mother-in-law and sisters-in-law that went back to the day of her birth. In the event of disagreement with her husband, it was very often he who had to give way before the

26. Pierre de Beaumont, *Du temps de la Mère-Dame*, Paris, p. 62 (title appearing in the Basic French series).

27. Léopold Génicot, 'La noblesse au Moyen Age dans l'ancienne "Francie"', *Annales, Economies, Sociétés, Civilisations*, January/February 1962, p. 5: 'But though there is no biological continuity...is there not a continuity of concepts?'

28. In the endogamous societies where I have spent most time (Aurès), the group within which people married by preference might number from one hundred to three hundred individuals (*ferqa*), and the group outside which they almost never married (tribe) rarely exceeded a thousand individuals.

invincible coalition of the feminine bloc, and I have known boys, married without their wishes having been consulted, flee to France to escape a wife whom they did not dare repudiate.[29] In this situation, polygamy was exceptional, even repudiation became less frequent and less arbitrary, and one *never* saw a child abandoned by its father.

Before her marriage, the girl had of course seen her male cousins, without having to wear a cowl. And she had naturally spoken with them, often at close quarters. Obviously, too, they in principle respected her: her honour was dear to them, for it was their own. Nevertheless, in certain regions of the Maghreb (precisely the most archaic), tolerance between relatives is great; and even in those regions where morality is strictest, nature, soft grass, chance... In short, in any society sooner or later everything will happen. When the event takes place within an endogamous tribe, however, no one mentions it. Over-susceptible girls are married to whichever cousin they prefer. Widows and divorced women lead a not-too-austere life, without arousing disapproval. Only married women are obliged to observe a certain restraint, itself less absolute than might at first sight appear. Among certain mountain peoples of the Atlas, in particular, when a husband is away for weeks on end, nobody is shocked at his leaving his wife alone with the shepherd (it is true that the latter is very often a cousin). Belief in the 'Bou-Mergoud' (literally 'sleeping child') is only a complement to this ancient tolerance: as we all know, this obliges a man who has been away for several years to recognize the child his wife may have borne in the meantime as his own. We all know too that this solace offered to abandoned wives has received the backing of Muslim law.

---

29. One of them was the first man from the Beni-Melkem tribe to come and work in France (in 1937). The eldest son of a widow, he had been so furious to have this marriage imposed on him that he had not attended the festivities. The marriage was valid nonetheless. Not daring to repudiate his wife, out of respect for his mother, he had gone off 'so that she would grow bored and leave'. After a year of solitude, the abandoned wife did indeed end up by leaving and, overjoyed, the husband sent back the deed confirming his repudiation of her. In the meantime, he had earned a great deal of money; he then returned and married a wife of his own choosing.

So the married woman must be faithful, but in an endogamous *douar*, if by some mischance she is not, the husband/cousin has a choice between two solutions: to repudiate her with no fuss, or to kill his cousin/rival. If he takes vengeance, this will not expose him to counter-vengeance from his victims' kinsmen, for they are his own kinsmen too and will generally reckon that one dead man in the family is enough. At most, in tribes where private property is long established, he will pay the 'blood-price'.

In addition to this freedom in relations within a warm environment, women enjoy numerous considerations in many nomadic Arab tribes,[30] even though, let us not forget, descent among them is exclusively patrilineal. Thus the Ouled Saoula, a Saharan tribe from the Zab Chergui which I knew some twenty years ago, still specified in their marriage contracts that no woman of their blood could go up a certain hill on foot; so to preserve them from any fatigue a white camel and a slave-girl had to be included in their marriage-portion.[31] By this time the Ouled Saoula were much too poor to have camels or serving-girls, but they went on writing these clauses into the deeds. Proud, touchy men, they married women of their own blood, and forgave each other as one cousin/brother to another for lapses in protocol—perhaps, when they could, offering the 'sister/wife' a she-ass for climbing too-steep hillocks.

'Warn the Dummy Not to Drink All the Milk'

Among nomads in Mauritania, favoured by political chance and a kinder climate, the considerations accorded to women are still governed by custom. The young bride belonging to a well-off family in effect receives both a marriage-portion from her husband and a dowry from her father. The latter always includes a tent,

---

30. Some nomads who speak Berber—the Tuareg—have a matrilineal kinship system. Here 'Arab' is taken to mean 'Arabic-speaking'.
    31. The marriage-portion (or sum paid by the husband to his wife on the occasion of their wedding) is a Koranic obligation. Often it is paid only in part, or even not paid at all, as is the case here. See note 34 below.

sometimes one or more slaves,[32] together with livestock, which she may dispose of as she pleases. She often requires her husband to accept a contractual obligation to repudiate her—with an exorbitant portion—if he takes a second wife; he will, moreover, pay this in full only in the event of divorce: in other words, if one fine day he decides to conclude another marriage. This clause constitutes a very effective safeguard against polygamy, and a relative safeguard against repudiation. During the first months of marriage, the young wife continues to live near her father's encampment, in the white tent that was an offering from her kinfolk. There it is that the new husband comes to visit her like a bashful lover, until she agrees to come and live with him, generally after the birth of their first child.

In everyday life, not only will a man of good family refrain from directing any reproach at his wife, but politeness will also debar him from directing any at her slaves (if she has any of her own). The Moors jokingly recount the following story. A man is expecting guests and, of course, would like to receive them lavishly. But he never has any milk left, because his wife's servant steals it every day. 'I am expecting guests tomorrow', the courteous husband tells the slave, 'so warn the dummy today not to drink all the milk.' In many nomadic countries—and Mauritania is a prime example—in order to encourage lactation, it is customary to place a straw-filled dummy representing her calf alongside a she-camel one wishes to milk. In the Ahaggar, I was told that this practice is adopted only when the calf has died. Its hide is then removed, stuffed with straw, sewn up, and placed near the she-camel, so that she will allow

---

32. Slavery is officially forbidden in Africa. This has been the case in the former French colonies since 1909 (by which time, however, more than fifty years had elapsed since the government passed the decree banning it in 1848); in Nigeria since 1916; in Sierra Leone since 1928. See on this subject Vincent Monteil, *L'Islam noir*, Paris 1964, p. 251. In practice, slavery still survives in the Sahara territories. As a result of official prohibitions, slaves can be bought or sold only exceptionally and illegally. On the other hand, their masters do what they please with them, pay them no wages, and can give them away. The survival of slavery is one of the most tragic problems of the Sahara, but it is an economic rather than a juridical or political one. Juridically, the slaves are free; but they will be *actually* free only when they can be provided with paid employment, and when the society in which they live acknowledges their freedom.

herself to be milked in the belief that her offspring is still alive. After five months the dummy is thrown away, because the untanned hide is serviceable only for the period of a single lactation. She-camels, in fact, supposedly recognize their own offspring and do not allow themselves to be duped by the hide of any old calf. I have been told that in Mali the Aoulimidden Tuareg do the same thing with cows that have lost their calves. But it is not apparently done with ewes or nanny-goats. In the Ahaggar, the dummy is called *ahayoudj* (plural: *iheoudien*).[33]

The Nomadic Clan

To complete this picture of the nomadic clan, we must point out that strictly speaking it is possible to observe religious law within it—in other words, to give wives a marriage-portion and daughters an inheritance—without thereby destroying the entire architecture of the society.[34] The patrimony, in fact, is made up almost entirely of livestock, and when it does include land this is cultivated directly only by slaves. It is, therefore, possible to make deductions from the inheritance, if this becomes necessary, without forcing the family to accept neighbourly relations and thus compromise its

---

33. In a book that makes an extremely valuable contribution to study of the Tuareg (*Ecology and Culture of the Pastoral Tuareg*, Copenhagen 1963, pp. 57 etc.), Johannes Nicolaisen writes: 'All Tuareg and perhaps all camel-rearing Arabs make use of the sown-up hide of a dead camel-calf to milk the animal's mother during the lactation period, since she-camels, like cows, will generally not give any milk if their young are not there. This custom is widespread among stock-raisers in the Old World.' [Since the exact passage in question does not occur in the English original of Nicolaisen's study, it has been retranslated here from the French version quoted by G.T.—*Translator's note.*] The anecdote above was told me in Mauritania seven years ago by a Moor of the Beni Hassan, that is, an Arabic-speaker.

34. In the Algerian west and in part of Morocco, well-off Muslim families and many poor ones voluntarily give their daughters a set of furniture upon marriage. This gift, which must accordingly be called a *dowry*, is not obligatory and will one day be deducted from the inheritance; the latter, however, is a religious obligation. In addition, the husband *must* give his wife a sum of money or its equivalent in jewelry as a marriage-portion. This obligatory marriage-portion lies behind the legend bandied about in certain ill-informed or ill-intentioned milieux that Muslim women are bought by their husbands. Naturally, an institution may always degenerate: the marriage-portion may be taken by the father, excessively inflated, or paid by some rich old man (a common occurrence in towns). On the other hand, it may be reduced to a symbolic sum (Aurès and Kabylia).

principles. With sedentary peasants, by contrast, where the patrimony is made up of fields, acceptance of religious law has the inevitable result, sooner or later, of destroying the unity of the tribal lands, and hence of the tribal structure.

Among Tuareg nomads—where traces of matrilineal descent survive almost everywhere—one would expect to find even more striking consideration accorded to women than in Mauritania. But one finds nothing of the kind: indeed, there is a very close resemblance between the two nomadic societies, Tuareg and Arab. On this point as on others, the differences between matrilineal and patrilineal structures are slight. In particular, the Koranic legislation protecting women is strictly observed in both regions.

The Koran in fact requires that the daughter receive a portion of her parents' inheritance,[35] and that upon marriage the husband give his wife a sum of money, which she will often offer to her father, convert into traditional gifts, or use herself as she pleases. But except among the Tuareg and the Moors, in rural areas throughout Arab-Berber Africa *religious law is everywhere violated* on these two points. What makes this all the more worthy of mention is that other African Muslims invariably flaunt their devoutness and openly despise Tuareg lack of orthodoxy.

The truth is that the two societies—the nomadic society of the Sahara and the sedentary society—did not offer equal resistance to religious erosion on this precise point. The moment has now come to seek to evaluate this resistance, for wind and storm assault granite as they do silt, but they do not act upon them in the same way.

---

35. See section of the following chapter entitled 'The Koranic Revolution'.

7
Conflict With God

A Selective Piety

The influences that have so far caused tribal society in the Maghreb to evolve have been contact with cities, religion, great wealth, extreme poverty and, over-population. To these will no doubt soon be added education, television, and politics, though these latter causes of mutation have operated only in the towns, while in the countryside their effects will not be felt for a few years yet. As for administrative committees and political parties, they have as yet no influence upon family structures. The evolutionary process began in the twilight of history—long before Moses, long before Jesus, long before Muhammad. But like a rust or oxidization, it first acted only at the surface, wherever there was contact between the society of field and steppe and that of the towns. With religion, it was finally to attempt penetration of the tribes in depth.

A good exercise for the mind, and a way of getting inside the skin of a civilization, is to compare a society's real mores with the prescriptions of its morality and religion, and then to measure the gap between them. Just as the old societies of Europe picked and chose from Christianity what served to consolidate their positions (omitting or disguising anything whose effect would have been to correct their essential failings), so the societies of Africa and Asia Minor subjected Islam to the same kind of treatment. This will allow us to distinguish two categories in the prescriptions of the Koran: first, admonitions that have generally been observed and even carried to excess (for example, those regarding the veil); second, a whole gamut of peremptory commands that have been stubbornly ignored over the centuries, and this category basically contains the *religious* precepts whose aim is to give women individual rights.

The Muslim faith—last-born of the three great monotheistic creeds, but issuing from the same Semitic crater—nearly covered over the lava deposited by the two previous eruptions, in the area where they originated. And in that northern region of the Levantine peninsula where all three came into the world, it so happens that the religions of a Single God necessarily encountered a milieu long unsettled by the 'structural collapse' whose symptoms we shall be analysing in the next chapter.[1]

First-born of the three, the religion of Israel swarmed far from its place of origin, into alien continents in which, ever in a minority, it should normally have been expected to melt away. It survived, however, thanks probably to the persecution of which its devotees were the victims: if there are still 'Jews', it is perhaps because of 'anti-semites'. As for Christianity, partly submerged by Islam in its own place of birth, it was to find its chosen terrain (and a majority position) in countries influenced by Germanic law,[2] which from earliest antiquity has accorded women the juridical status of individuals. In short, Islam was almost alone in 'mopping up' a social phenomenon whose relationship with it resulted essentially from geography, not from theology.

The Veil According to St. Paul

Until quite recently—before the tourist boom of the fifties and early sixties, to be precise—a woman caused a scandal if she entered a church in Spain, Portugal, the south of France, Corsica, southern Italy, Greece, or Lebanon without having her head covered, at least by a handkerchief. It is true that one of St. Paul's Epistles advocates this.[3] But St. Paul also abjures slaves to be obedient to their

---

1. See the section of chapter 8 entitled 'Seven Thousand Years of Destroying the Old Structures'.
2. This is less true for Catholics than for Protestants.
3. The First Epistle of Paul the Apostle to the Corinthians, chapter 11. Without being a specialist in St. Paul's writings, it is easy to distinguish two veins of inspiration in his epistles: the more important of these brings us the reflections of an original, profound, and timeless meditation; this, however, is juxtaposed with the

masters 'as unto Christ'[4]—and Christian slaves have nevertheless forsaken slavery. He likewise counsels the renunciation of vengeance: 'Bless them which persecute you: bless, and curse not.... Recompense to no man evil for evil.... Dearly beloved, avenge not yourselves,...'[5]—yet the north of the Mediterranean, until our grandparents' generation, remained almost universally faithful to the vendetta (that is, the *moral duty* to avenge oneself and avenge all members of one's family), and if in the Christian countries the vendetta is now falling into disuse here and there, it is not out of obedience to St. Paul, since religious practice very often suffers a similar fate. In the same period, bare-headed women were no shock in the churches of Paris or Rheims[6]—though St. Paul is no less revered there than in the chapels of Bastia or Taranto. The 'mental sieve' of Christians north of the Loire, receiving the same Word, evidently did not retain the same words as the Mediterranean sieve.

Joan of Arc and Robert the Pious

Marcel Mauss often used to insist, in his lectures at the Collège de France, upon the following difference between Roman and Germanic law: in the former, the mother had a kinship relation with her son only because, by a legal fiction, *she was considered an elder sister*; but in the latter, as in most present-day European legal

---

everyday conversation of an active, busy man from the first century of our epoch. It is the busy man who speaks to us of the veil, for here is what he says: 'For a man indeed ought not to cover his head, forasmuch as he is the image and glory of God: but the woman is the glory of the man...neither was the man created for the woman,...for this cause ought the woman to have a [a sign of] power on her head because of the angels.'

4. The Epistle of Paul the Apostle to the Ephesians, chapter 6, verse 5. In spite of St. Paul's advice, slavery disappeared progressively in Western Europe around the eleventh century—for social and economic reasons, not religious ones. South of the Mediterranean, the situation is the exact opposite. There the Koran explicitly recommends the freeing of Muslim slaves, yet slavery has been sporadically maintained to this very day: openly in Saudi Arabia, clandestinely in the Saharan areas of the Maghreb. In both cases, the causes that have operated have been exclusively economic. See note 32, chapter 6.

5. The Epistle of Paul the Apostle to the Romans, chapter 12, verses, 14, 17 and 19.

6. I saw a notice recently, in a church in Britanny, warning women not to enter in shorts.

codes, the son was kin to both his father and his mother. Mauss used to point out in this regard that when Robert the Pious married a descendant of Charlemagne to legitimize his rights, it was because he considered that the land of France was not Salic. Consequently, in the dispute that gave rise to the Hundred Years War, the law and the juridical tradition of the kings of France favoured the English claim. In favour of the French claim, there was Joan of Arc and what is nowadays called 'national identity'. The 'nordic' influence makes itself felt in France, even in the southern part of the country. Thus for quite a long time now women have not been forcibly married, nor secluded or veiled. The industrial power of the northern states, moreover, has contributed to disseminating their customs in all the Mediterranean countries. So France, Italy, Yugoslavia, and Greece have finally granted women political rights.[7] In Portugal these rights came with the 1974 revolution, and in Spain women won political rights when men did, after the death of Franco.

Our Holy Mother Church Is a Masculine Mother

The reverse influence also operates. In France, even in the north of the country, the Mediterranean directs social customs—through the medium of Roman law, the Catholic Church, and the Napoleonic Code. Only a few years ago, married women were still legally considered minors, and found themselves in the same situation *vis-à-vis* their husbands as children *vis-à-vis* their fathers, unable to request a passport or a bank account without a husband's authorization.[8] Since the 1974 reform, however, fathers and mothers exert their authority in common during a marriage; after a divorce, the paternal power is transferred to whoever has custody of the child; and if a departure abroad is involved, the father or mother can oppose this after a court ruling.

---

7. In Switzerland, women won the right to vote at the federal level very recently, but at the cantonal level two German-speaking districts still denied them that right in the late 1970s. The Principality of Liechtenstein and the Republic of San Marino also figure among the last bastions of 'politically conscious phallocracy'.

8. The Canadian government had granted such rights at the federal level back in 1918, but: 'It is in fact noteworthy that the province of Quebec has never elected a

Since the French Revolution, daughters have inherited from their parents on the same basis as sons: yet whole books could be filled simply by noting the way French laws are violated daily, to the detriment of women, in most parts of the country. It is tacitly accepted, in many regions, that the family land and house should go to the eldest son.[9] For this reason, and so that they may be more easily attributed to him, they are normally assessed at a quarter of their value when the estate is apportioned. Since magistrates, notaries, and tax-collectors all consider this tacit clause highly moral, they apply it by common agreement: it is thus thanks to them that French 'domains' have been partially conserved. The same is true with industrial firms: at the founder's death, an apportionment is made among all his heirs of 'shares' that yield no income and may not be sold; this allows the sons, always endowed with more or less real functions in the family business, to arrogate to themselves the totality of the profits in the form of salaries—to the detriment of their (sometimes beloved) sisters who, so as to comply with the law, are given a few symbolic, unusable pieces of paper representing their inheritance.

These phenomena merely reflect a family hierarchy that is still well preserved in France, especially south of the Loire. Countless anecdotes could be mentioned in connection with this: for example, that excellent father, intellectual, and rich bourgeois from the Midi who, in 1964, thought it natural to take a first-class sleeping-berth for his son (a strapping youth), while making his daughters travel second class on the same train.

The status of women in Europe thus appears marked by an archaic nordic, liberal tradition opposed, over the centuries, by three Mediterranean influences: that of Roman law; that of the Napoleonic Code (whose architect, let us not forget, was a Corsican); and that of traditional Catholicism. For Our Holy Mother Church has remained a 'masculine mother' to this day. In 1962, for example, at the great universal assembly known as Vatican II,

---

single woman to the provincial or federal governments, whereas almost all the other Canadian provinces have done so.' (Article by Guy Rocher in P.-H. Chombart de Lauwe (ed.), *Images de la femme dans la société*, Paris 1964, p. 200.)

9. On primogeniture, see chapter 5 above.

no abbess was admitted to deliberate with the 2,200 Conciliar Fathers. 'Women may not be priests', Catholics reply. Yet even at the time when popes used to raise laymen or young children to the rank of cardinal, none of them ever considered conferring the purple upon a woman: the very idea is absurd! The solemn positions adopted by all those celibate men with respect to birth-control gave added confirmation of the very Italian archaism of the Catholic apparatus.

For reasons at once geographical and historical, it happens that in Muslim society this status has almost everywhere met an exactly opposite situation: mores more retrograde than religion.

The Koranic Revolution

In the seventh century of our epoch, Islam embarked upon a *practical* struggle against the infamies spreading through Arab society undergoing urbanization—and not only against those infamies, but also against their deeper causes.[10] Among the infamies in question must be classified debasement of the condition of women; and among the causes of that debasement certainly figured, even then, the 'collapse of old structures' and the defensive reaction engendered by such a collapse: the veritable social allergy we alluded-ed to right back in the first chapter of this book. It must be attributed to the artificial maintenance, in towns and villages, of obligations elaborated in the nomadic clans of western Asia and North Africa.

With respect to inheritance, here is what Islamic law prescribes. Each orphaned girl shall be given a portion of her father's goods

---

10. The Muslim has to obey a certain number of rules that are difficult to observe, but not impossible. Such obedience can lead those who submit to it wholeheartedly to become 'perfect Muslims', men who know peace. At the centre of their meditation shines forth the unity of God, which is not a source of anguish, since God is beyond compare. The message of Christ, by contrast, is atemporal; according to his own words, his kingdom is not of this world, so it does not much matter if there are slaves (thought the first Christians), since what counts is salvation. The Christian message is so far from being 'practical' that in no time or place has there been a state fully applying the precepts of the Gospels. Furthermore, for the true Christian, Christ is a real and conceivable model, ever present to the heart, but at the same time inaccessible, since he represents a demand for perfection that no man can

equal to half that of a male child, and half the entire inheritance if there are no sons (the remainder being shared between the dead man's widow, ascendants, and brothers). To the widow: a quarter of her husband's estate if he has no descendants, otherwise an eighth. To the ascendants (if the dead man still has any) the law accords equal portions: either a third to the father and a third to the mother, if the dead man has no son; or else, a sixth to each of them.[11] To appreciate just how reasonable this division was, in the social context in which it was promulgated, we must remember that the Koran charges the husband with full responsibility for maintaining his wife and children, however poor he may be or however rich his wife. In addition, it endows the married woman with *independent* management of her personal goods (dowry, marriage-portion, and inheritance).[12]

In this perspective, the lawgiver consequently had to provide for the upkeep not only of each son, but also eventually of the latter's wife and children. Each daughter, by contrast, could rely on the maintenance that her husband—and later her son—were bound by law to afford her. In no circumstances was she to have responsibility for meeting needs other than her own.[13] Indeed, for her to be reduced even to that, she would have to be pursued by a series of disasters: in other words, she would have to be unlucky enough to find herself at once widow, orphan, and without either son or

---

attain and that nonetheless cannot be eluded. This is why there can be good Christians, but no perfect Christians, save one: Jesus.

11. *The Koran*, translated by N. J. Dawood, Harmondsworth 1981, p. 367 (Sura 4, 'On Women', verse 12).

12. The Catholic Church, for its part, has tried to protect women by formally prohibiting divorce and polygamy; however, though it of course condemns adultery and murder, it is sometimes prepared to pardon them, with the consequence that these not very commendable procedures are used in Christian countries to 'alleviate' monogamy. The Koran, meanwhile, advises against divorce and authorizes polygamy, but on conditions that in practice are never fulfilled (in particular, all the wives must be treated with absolute equality); on the other hand, it reserves all its severity for adultery. In reality, there is little polygamy in the traditional countries of the Maghreb, very little adultery, a great deal of divorce, and no bastard children (few are born, and those who are born do not live: in plain terms, infanticide). Thus each country has its own misdeeds and crimes, as a dark reverse side of its virtues.

13. Until the last few years, this was true throughout rural areas of the Maghreb. In the towns and villages, women abandoned with all their children by the father are now very numerous, and more numerous every day.

brother able to take her in. And if such were the case, she ought to have half her father's estate, a quarter of her husband's, and the wedding-portion bestowed upon her when she married.

At the time of the Koranic revelation, these precepts represented the most 'feminist' legislation in the civilized world. But in a homogeneous tribe it constituted a veritable explosive charge—and still does.

Among town burghers, when the patrimony is made up of pieces of material or bags of money, it will not be impossible to give each son and each daughter the portion of the father's, son's, or husband's goods granted them expressly by religious law. *Nevertheless, thanks to this law the great urban fortunes of Islam are more rarely maintained, and with more difficulty, than great Christian fortunes.*

Among nomads, too, it is possible to share out the she-camels, ewes, and goats, according to the same scale of reckoning: but it is worth trying to picture the operation in practice. Let us suppose a Bedouin dies before his mother, leaving to his two sons, his three daughters, and his widow an inheritance made up of forty-eight sheep. According to religious law, six have to go to the widow, eight to the mother, five to each of the three daughters and ten to each of the boys—making, for anyone who can count, forty-nine sheep in all. Each of the three daughters really has a right only to 4.95 sheep, each son to 9.90 sheep, and so on. In practice, matters are arranged by giving a fat lamb, for example, or a one-eyed ewe, in settlement of the fraction of an animal owed to so-and-so. But in fact things are arranged more smoothly since arguing is just *not done*—it is considered bad manners. If, however, by some mischance there should be a dispute, the Law would then be interpreted by the *qadi* or by an ancient senate (the *jema'a*[14]) made up of the family headsmen who run the tribe or village, and that is probably how they would settle the estate.

In practice, except in the (very rare) event of conflict, the flock will not be divided. For the grandmother would live very badly, alone with her eight sheep. The widow (very often the mother of

---

14. I have seen one functioning in Pakistan, identical to those I knew in the Aurès, in Kabylia, in the Ouarsenis, in the Moroccan Atlas.

some, if not all, of the children) would be still less well provided for, with the six that fall to her share. Moreover, mother, grandmother, and sisters are all afraid of living alone and feel the need of some protection; and they have a right to that of the man who is their brother, son, or grandson. If there is no inheritance, they will confidently rely on him to share with them the meagre rewards of his labour—and formerly he would never have dared disappoint that reliance. So the *eldest* son[15] will be seen to arrange everything, just as his father used to do, without any change apparently affecting the distribution of property. Yet everyone knows what belongs to this man or that woman.

Among sedentary agriculturists everything is different since it is no longer animals, coins, or cubits of material being divided up, but *fields*. The peasant who dies leaving a holding of forty-eight hectares to be shared between the seven heirs enumerated above must cut out of his land an enclave of twenty-odd hectares destined for his daughters and wife. But these daughters may marry men from another lineage, another *ferqa*, another village. Their children will then be foreigners, and these foreigners will one day take possession of their maternal grandfather's hectares, which will then cease to belong to people of the same name. In the case of the Maghreb peasant, religious practice thus destabilizes a society that is entirely constructed upon the homogeneity of the family holding, and upon the impossibility for any man bearing a name other than that of the group to install himself upon it, without first being adopted 'as a brother'.[16] The tomb of the eponymous ancestor, moreover, is almost always there—on the highest or most central spot—to symbolize the appropriation of the soil by his lineage.

'...Into Hell-fire and Shall Abide in It for Ever'

The apportionment laid down by the Koran thus poses problems that go beyond a simple tally of possessions. In a literal sense, the question is one not of *having* but of *being*. For the man who

---

15. See the section entitled 'My Lord Brother' of chapter 5 above.
16. See the section above entitled 'Joint Honour', and what Herodotus says about pacts of brotherhood (p. 85 above).

violates the law concerning inheritance, the Holy Book, which so often alludes to divine compassion, offers nothing to soften a merciless severity: there is no room for interpretation, no possible escape-clause or ambiguity. Let us simply open the Koran (Sura 4, verse 13), where we read, after the list of rules, the following phrase word for word: 'He that defies Allah...shall be cast into Hell-fire and shall abide in it for ever.' We should not forget, moreover, that with these old peasant populations of the Maghreb, we are in a fortress of Islam, amidst people bursting with faith, for whom the truths revealed by the Prophet are not symbols: what is being referred to is real Fire, and a real Eternity in that Fire.

Let us next consider the cadastral situation in the Maghreb.[17] We shall find that for thirteen centuries, at a rate of three generations per century, the peasants of the Maghreb—all devout Muslims, it goes without saying—have opted for hell-fire rather than sacrifice the appropriation of their land by their lineage. And as for those tribes that over the ages preferred to save their everlasting souls, they sacrificed for the latter what they held most dear: their survival in this world.

Just for the sake of comparison, it is worth mentioning here the very mild sanctions the Holy Book of Islam envisages for those who break the Ramadan fast (Sura 2): 'he who is ill or on a journey shall fast a similar number of days later on....for those that can afford it there is a ransom: the feeding of a poor man....Allah desires your well-being, not your discomfort.'[18] Quite recently, a Muslim doctor told me how he had found a seriously wounded man by a roadside. After treating him, he learnt not without indignation that his patient had been beaten up and left lying there by his own village, for the crime of violating the Ramadan fast. This was a village in the Constantine region where, for almost a thousand years, from father to son, the 'Eternity in the Flames' promised inexorably to men who deprive women of their inheritance had been contemplated with the most perfect equanimity.

---

17. I have done this is in the Aurès, in Greater and Lesser Kabylia, and in highland Morocco.
18. *The Koran*, p. 351 (Sura 2, verses 184–5).

Matrilineal Descent and Orthodoxy

In the far south of the Sahara, the Maghreb still contains a branch of the Berbers (the most archaic still extant today) in which kinship in the mother's line has been maintained. Not everywhere: among Tuareg of the South-East (Aïr) in particular, succession now passes chiefly from father to son—but even in that region, a detailed study shows that the extent of matrilineal kinship, at a relatively recent date, was much greater than it is today.[19] Three rapid surveys I carried out myself over a period of nine years allowed me likewise to record an effective weakening of this system of descent in the Ahaggar, especially at Djanet.[20] Matrilineal descent among Berbers is not limited, moreover, to the Tuareg: it has also been recorded in another branch—the Gouanche—which died out during historical times.[21]

Today, only privileges still follow the female line, where it subsists. These privileges, of course, include royal power, but also clan name, social status, hunting rights. Nowadays, the father's status increasingly influences that of the child, but this seems to be a recent phenomenon. On the other hand, for a long time—as far back as the oral tradition goes—the child has borne as a second name that of his father, and the wife comes to live in her husband's household.

Well nowadays, in all Tuareg areas, chattels and real estate forming part of an inheritance are apportioned according to the most orthodox Muslim law: two shares to the sons, one to the daughters. The anomaly here, in comparison with other Berber regions, consists precisely in not monkeying with religious law. All authors who have described the Tuareg have invariably been only too glad to emphasize that which is non-Muslim in their way of life: 'they have innumerable superstitions', 'they do not say their prayers', 'they do

---

19. Studies carried out between 1951 and 1959 by the Dane Johannes Nicolaisen (see note 33, chapter 6).
20. During three short stays, in 1956, 1961, and 1965.
21. Georges Marcy, 'Les vestiges de la parenté maternelle en droit coutumier berbère et le régime des successions touarègues', *Revue Africaine* LXXXV (3rd and 4th quarters, 1941), pp. 186–211.

not fast', and so on. Nothing of all this is false, but all the same it is
less true than it was five years ago, and less true every day. Let us,
however, concede this point of view, which has been that of all
observers of the Tuareg without exception. Lo and behold, then,
on one point—that question of inheritance to which the Koran attaches so much importance—our pagan Tuareg apply the law strictly, unanimously, and without flinching, while all the rest of the
devout Maghreb has been busy violating it for a thousand years.

To understand this unexpected orthodoxy, we must refer back to
the chapter on honour and nobility.[22] For in a land of maternal descent, as in one of paternal descent, it is essential not to dislocate
society by 'breaking' the clan. And one breaks the clan by letting
land go to outsiders: in other words, to the children of sons when
the name and race are transmitted by women, to the children of
daughters when the transmission is from father to son. In Tuareg
areas, the problem was not posed as in the northern Maghreb,
because land is not private property among the Tuareg: it belongs
to the sovereign (in the Ahaggar), or to the *taousit* (tribe) in certain
agricultural centres such as Djanet. For this reason, inheritance in
both lines did not risk 'breaking' tribal unity. In addition, religious
law here corresponded to a heartfelt wish, since natural feelings
conflict more strongly with descent in the female than with descent
in the male line. This does not mean that a Kabyle unlucky enough
to have only daughters will accept with good grace seeing all his
property go to his nephew, while his daughters have nothing. But
the nephew and heir will usually be his son-in-law, which makes
things easier, and will always have been brought up near his paternal uncle, who will have grown accustomed to considering him a
son. And a real son is never in any circumstances disappointed,
since if he exists it is always he who inherits.

In a system in which the clan is patrilocal (as is presently the case
among the Tuareg), but in which inheritance is transmitted through
the female line, from maternal uncle to sister's son (as seems to
have been their former custom[23]), things happen quite differently.

---

22. Chapter 6, 'Nobility According to Averroës and Nobility According to Ibn
Khaldun'.
23. Nicolaisen, p. 174.

The father brings up his children and keeps them near him, though he knows that when he dies they will have to leave his encampment and go to live in their mother's family. Meanwhile his true kin—his sister's children—are brought up by brothers-in-law who may, of course, also be his cousins, but not necessarily so. In practice, such a man risks having as his heir a boy who not only is not his son, but who has been brought up far away from him as well. An old Tuareg proverb I recorded in the Ahaggar in 1965 says of the sister's son, approximately, that he 'eats' his maternal uncle's property but defends his honour.[24] And indeed, that is the only point in common between these two men: honour, a name.

A Transfer Back to God, by Notarized Deed

At Djanet (where all land belongs to the village), an Arab married to a Tuareg woman may plant palm-trees half of which will belong to him, and may choose the heirs to his portion in accordance with the Koran. If the trees are sold, they will get half the price; if the trees are cut down, they will have half the wood. But whatever happens, the land will sooner or later return to its owner, in this case the village. If the planter of the trees is a local man, he will at once give them to his wife,[25] who ten years ago would immediately have a *habous* drawn up to disinherit her sons[26] (just as a Berber from the North would have been anxious to disinherit his daughters). Whichever sex is disinherited, the motive remains the same: to preserve the unity of the holding.

In order to 'legally violate the law', as soon as he bought a piece of land, the father of a family in Lesser Kabylia or the Aurès would make haste to have a deed drawn up by the *qadi* stipulating that he had chosen God as his ultimate heir: however, pending such time as

---

24. *Ag-alet-ma-K netta ainagan ibendja-enna K, imaKchi nahagh-ennaK*: the son of thy mother's daughter, he slays thine enemy, he eats thy property.

25. A man from Djanet plants palm-trees only to pay the marriage-portion for a wife.

26. The *habous* is a deed of donation to God, and there are many pious foundations in the Maghreb that have not been diverted from their vocation. A deed of donation to God, in which the latter is designated only as the 'ultimate heir', is termed a 'private *habous*'. All the heirs named by the testator have to enter into possession of the property before Him.

the 'Great Heir' might take possession of His property, enjoyment of it was to be reserved exclusively for his male descendants. I should also make it clear that in the part of the Aurès where I was doing field work between 1934 and 1940, apart from a field recently bought by a man having only daughters, there was not a single piece of land that was not covered by a *habous* of this kind.

In practice, we may distinguish three types of evolution with respect to female inheritance in the greater Maghreb. In the *first category* the Koran is applied, in which case we are dealing with very devout people, nomads of matrilineal descent (Ahaggar). In the *second category* the Koran is violated, but some trouble is taken to try to deceive God, by making Him the heir—by this we may recognize the Aurès or Lesser Kabylia. In the *third category* there is no *habous*, no Koran, nothing for the daughters, and nothing for God—we are now among the men of Greater Kabylia.

In Islam, as in Christianity, Mediterranean woman has regularly been despoiled. On the one hand, despite the French Revolution, on the other despite the Koran. In France, such despoliation survives nowadays only in residual areas. But the reason for this evolution is to be sought in a general economic progress, which brings all else in its wake, in particular increasingly destroying 'family property' and inducing an ever growing number of women to embark on careers. In all this, religion and morality have played *no role whatever*. Islam, in contrast to Christianity, has tackled the problem head on, and with a lack of success worth underlining. Muslims, or at least large numbers of them, have blatantly violated divine precepts. Some, with true peasant guile, have sought to make God himself an accomplice in their disobedience, by 'transferring back' their inheritance to Him through a notarized deed, but to be taken possession of only on Judgement Day.

The Geographical Distribution of the Veil
Corresponds to Female Inheritance

Given the damage caused by tribal disintegration, or more accurately by the reactions this provoked, two positions had been possible: the traditionalist one consisted in struggling against that disintegration; the revolutionary one had to strive to bring it swiftly to completion. In making inheritance by women obligatory, the Holy Book opted very firmly for the second solution. It thus struck a terrible blow at the tribe: a blow that tribal societies, even as with more or less good grace they converted to Islam, have bent their energies to evading ever since. And not without some success, as we have seen, since they still survive.

We can see today that the geographical distribution of the veil, and of female seclusion, corresponds roughly to respect for the Koran on the question of inheritance by women. Beneath the outward show of pious submission, this seems in fact to be a protective mechanism: a last barrier raised against the damage wrought by religious observance in the patrimony of endogamous families. However, it does not represent the maximum degree of alienation. The maximum degree of alienation, for women, is encountered in mutant populations, ones detribalized by recent sedentarization or urbanization.

8

Bourgeois Snobbery[1]

Society in the Maghreb is still marked today by three compulsions. The most ancient, of which we spoke in chapter six ('Nobility According to Averroës and Nobility According to Ibn Khaldun'), goes back to prehistory and strives to preserve a lineage or race from any intermingling. Let us call it the 'noble' or 'Bedouin compulsion': flaunting itself in its proud solitude, it is nevertheless hopelessly condemned by the general evolution of the world. Next comes the peasant compulsion—the harshest—which is meant to maintain a particular kinship group upon a particular number of fields: it does not fear to oppose God himself, in the hearts of the owners of land (we followed and recounted the details and outcome of the conflict in the last chapter). Last comes the bourgeois compulsion—but in Muslim towns God wins; and yet there too the ideals of the old endogamous society survive.

We must not forget that urban evolution is more ancient in the Mediterranean Levant than anywhere else. But it seems as if it had continually been checked in mid course by a kind of thermostat.

---

1. The word 'snob', now international, originated as an English slang term, probably derived from a pun: for *sine nobilitate* (s.nob.) was contrasted in the great English public schools of the nineteenth century with *filius nobilis* (nob.), or lord's son; at the same time, 'snob' meant a cobbler. Taken up and made famous in 1848 by Thackeray in *The Book of Snobs*, the word had a great success. As for the situation it expresses, this belongs to every age and country, because there have always been elements of society that were changing. In our day, social instability, the great manufacturer of snobbery, is complemented by exhortations to 'Be different', which come from advertisements, the press, and television. See p. 159 below for the local bigshot nicknamed *cha-t-diya*. See too Pierre Daninos, *Snobissimo*, Paris 1964.

According to our hypothesis, this mechanism has functioned without a breakdown since neolithic times.

Seven Thousand Years of Destroying the Old Structures

The nucleus of the area we are concerned with corresponds fairly closely to the region in which, at the dawn of history, the Semitic, Hamitic, and Indo-European languages overlapped[2] (and others too, of course, which it has not been possible to classify, since they have not survived). It also corresponds to the region where the first towns appeared; where men for the first time sowed cereals,[3] led flocks to graze, shaped and baked a clay platter, wove a garment, polished a stone axe. There is no reason not to believe that the first town was initially a 'fortified tribe'. But the day certainly came fairly soon when it ceased to be a tribe and became a city—in other words, that crucible in which for more than seven thousand years 'old structures' were to be tirelessly destroyed and two societies were to stand face to face: the 'society of citizens' and the 'society of cousins'. We can reconstitute this uninterrupted destruction, this battle between adversaries never extirpated, since the phenomenon is still continuing before our eyes: it is our contemporary.

Those who find schematic constructions attractive (though one must not be too fond of them) will be tempted to see identification with a piece of land—which is characteristic of the oldest peasant populations of the Mediterranean South—as the first stage of tribal evolution. For to speak of 'peasants' is to think of 'tilling the soil', and there is no tilling without a village, no village without neighbours, and no neighbour without marriage to outsiders. In the subsequent phases of this schema we shall see the sedentary agriculturist become a villager, and then a citizen: stages of the same kind, since the transition from a nomadic to a sedentary way of life has itself represented, in less brutal terms, a sequence of destructions and readaptations analogous to those that characterize the transition from countryside to town.

---

2. The Assyrians spoke a Semitic language, ancient Egyptian is related to Hamitic, the Hittite language contains a significant Indo-European vocabulary, and ancient Persian civilization was Indo-European.

3. See, on this subject, chapters 2 and 4 above.

Today, during the last phase, contemporary geography textbooks all point to the accelerated, massive shift of rural populations into towns and villages: they have popularized the word 'urbanization' to designate this phenomenon. Sociologists and anthropologists, for their part, like to speak, in the same connection, of the 'destruction of old tribal structures'. They too are inexhaustible on the topic. The 'old structures' are indeed still collapsing, along all their frontiers, meaning wherever they come into contact with anything other than themselves. But they have been collapsing in this way ever since they had frontiers, in other words since they ceased to be men's only framework.

In practice, the opposition between 'old' and less old structures (but not therefore young) fairly often corresponds to a town/country opposition. So it is necessary to go back to the period in which urban life was born to find the source of the split and confrontation between the two systems. We have seen that it began a very long time before history; thanks to recent excavations and to the dating procedures afforded in particular by Carbon 14, it is now even possible to evoke the place and age in which it arose. For the moment, the doyen of towns seems to be the one that began on the site of ancient Jericho, near the Dead Sea. To be sure, new excavations will reveal still other ruins. But the multiplicity and coherence of the discoveries already made nevertheless make it possible to situate approximately, both in space and in time, one of the greatest human mutations: in time, from seven to nine thousand millennia before the atomic era; in space, a vast region bounded by three seas—the easternmost shore of the Mediterranean, the Caspian, the Red Sea. The 'old structures' are not yet entirely destroyed, since they continue to crumble before our eyes; but they began their decline more than seven thousand years ago (at least, in the part of the world where they survive).

Divergences Between History and Ethnography

In this part of the world, between the period of polished stone axes and the present epoch, numerous civilizations have succeeded one another: the longest series in history. Despotic, conquering civilizations, great creators of works of art and great pulverizers of peoples, characterized, the historian will tell us, by the inordinate valorization of a few families and the subordination of all the rest. Yet the ethnographer who traverses these same regions today encounters societies that *do not seem* to have been overturned, fragmented, flattened by thousands of years of active despotism—the reality of which, however, is attested by incontrovertible documents.

For the humblest families are proud, touchy, aggressive, and firmly anchored to autonomous structures that seem to have been preserved intact since the earliest antiquity and do not differ very much from 'noble' structures.

Should more importance be attached to what we *know* (namely history) than to what we *see* (ethnography)? In my view, it is a good idea to make full use of all the available data, and as it happens, what Mediterranean demography tells us makes this possible. For it is logical to think that 'oriental despotisms' weighed above all on sectors that were 'civilized', in other words heavily populated, which means irrigated, which in turn means urban: hence unquestionably sterilized by an infant-mortality almost equal to the birthrate, and moreover ravaged by epidemics not yet nipped in the bud by asepsis and antibiotics. It is no less logical to suppose that other populations coming from the savage plains or unconquered mountains then renewed the townsmen's blood, and simultaneously sacrificed their youth to the old ideals, which were perhaps beginning to be forsaken.

The Child-Devouring City

.This mechanism enables us to understand the phenomenon that lies at the very root of the Mediterranean's specificities: that is to say, the absurd maintenance of rural ideals within city walls.

In our own experience as twentieth-century Parisians, it is enough to consult the genealogies of our fellow citizens—or even the memories of the oldest among them—to realize that up to the end of the Second Empire all townsmen of ancient stock had among their eight great-grandparents at most one or two ancestors born in the capital. The fact can easily be explained, as we have seen, since the mortality rate was even greater in the towns than in the countryside; in particular, had it not been for constant immigration, infant mortality would have emptied all the cities. Until the twentieth century, indeed, the children of peasants or nomads everywhere in the world enjoyed a better 'chance of life' than city children. But in the great metropolises of Africa and Asia, where climate and overcrowding continually incubate the most deadly illnesses, the extermination of children was more radical than anywhere else. From the moment of their foundation, the huge mortality of the ancient cities obliged them constantly to attract numerous adults within their walls: only thus could they avoid disappearing for lack of inhabitants, and by remaining populous, remain also strong and wealthy. In the old countries of Europe, Africa, and Asia, the adults in question necessarily came from the neighbouring country tribes.[4]

This obligatory renewal was maintained unchanged until the great discoveries of modern medicine, which since Pasteur have called all the elements of an age-old equilibrium into question. (Let us be clear about this equilibrium: since it was based essentially upon the cruellest laws of nature, there is no reason to lament its passing. The biological imbalance that has now been established throughout the world, of course, does represent the most justifiable of reasons for humanity to be dismayed; but it is simultaneously the most imperative of incentives to progress.) In addition to its pitiless role as a regulator of births, this extermination of children (and the immigration that compensated for it) resulted in the maintenance, until the nineteenth century, of family relations between inhabitants of the countryside and inhabitants of the great cities, and consequently of all manner of comings and goings between street and field: especially marriages. All historians of our Middle Ages, and of the Arab Middle Ages likewise, have recorded these comings and goings.

---

4. In the new countries of America and Australia, it was to a great extent town-dwellers—or peasants who had first passed by way of the town—who went off to settle the land and create agriculture. French Canada is an exception, since it received the core of its present population in the seventeenth century, and this was made up of genuine peasants.

The Arrival of Adults Loaded Down With Convictions

The civilizing role of the town is such a cliché of sociology that etymologically the words used as antonyms for 'savage' all mean 'inhabitant of a city'.[5] In contrast to this familiar role, however, another of its functions—that of destroying and devouring human lives—deserved study, since until the nineteenth century this maintained what could be termed a 'country atmosphere' in all the world's great conurbations.

Until Pasteur, in fact, town-country relations can be represented in the shape of a two-way current. The numerically larger stream flows inexorably but silently from the countryside to the town. No organized, conspicuous human masses (or at least only rarely), but the continuous arrival of isolated individuals: adult individuals, in other words, people bearing a heavy burden of convictions. So in each generation these convictions are revitalized by new contributions, thanks to the immigrants. The other current flows in the opposite direction—from the town to the fields and grasslands—bearing conspicuous objects: books, fashions, ideas. It is registered in directories and catalogues, and thus leaves historical traces that will provide a feast for compilers, but it has neither strength nor depth, because very few men accompany it. Those who do, moreover, are transient officials: merchants, travellers, soldiers. Only the bearers of religious faith constitute an exception and settle.[6] For thousands

---

5. In English, as in French, the word 'civilization' is recent (eighteenth century); it comes from the verb 'to civilize', which comes from the word 'civil', which comes from the Latin *civis* (citizen), which also gave rise to *civitas* (citizenry) and thence to 'city' and 'citizen'.

6. The traces left by these evangelizing campaigns in the tribes of the Maghreb can be identified (especially by means of the genealogical method). We may first cite the almost contemporary preaching of the Ulama. Then, a century before (beginning of the nineteenth century), there had been a reimplantation of the marabout brotherhoods (particularly Rahmanya) that was still fresh in the Algerian countryside at the time of French conquest in 1830 (which explains why the marabouts then assumed leadership of the resistance). Three or four centuries earlier (fifteenth and sixteenth centuries), there was another series of implantations, especially in Greater and Lesser Kabylia. In a more distant past, the traces become imprecise in the oral tradition; it may nevertheless be wondered whether certain clans of the Ahmar Khaddou from the South, which call themselves *masmoûdi* (plural *msâmda*), might not be moraines left behind by the spread of the Almohade 'glaciation' (thirteenth century).

of years a rough balance ensured the survival of the two currents, the 'city' prospering thanks to the surplus of men surreptitiously drained off to it from steppe and hamlet. From time to time, a bigger wave swept through at ground level (which is the level of history) and ravaged the town: such a wave was called 'the end of a civilization'.

This pattern of growth and abundance followed by decadence and death was superimposed only too well upon the basic standard of measures and comparisons we all carry in our heads: human life from the cradle to the grave. Fine phrases automatically envelop a theme so well suited to them. In fact, however, though a 'Decline of the West' is not inconceivable, we no longer think that if our societies perish it will be due to an ageing of our structures or to the collective impoverishment of our vitality. The analogy with the ancient civilizations that succumbed militarily to the onrush of 'savages', like an old man before a young warrior, must henceforth be considered obsolete. Great dangers await the men of tomorrow, but these have no analogy with the dangers of which we have historical experience. It was, however, those Mediterranean historical models that caused Spengler to outline his blueprint for disaster, and caused Paul Valéry to write: 'We later civilizations... we too now know that we are mortal. We had heard tell of whole worlds that had vanished, of empires sunk without a trace.'[7]

In the town-country equilibrium of former times, the countryside was subjected to the influence of the towns. For in face of the organization and accumulation of knowledge, values, and means that every town represents, the countryside could only submit and be subjected, not only to ways of thinking, but often also to civil order and all that it implies. The living substance, on the other hand, was supplied by the countryside to the town, thus influencing the latter intimately and secretly. And without that substance, the town would have disappeared.

---

7. 'The Crisis of the Mind' (1919), in Paul Valéry, *History and Politics (Collected Works*, vol. 10), London 1963, p. 23.

Half-Way Through an Evolution

I have had the opportunity to personally get to know many people who have lived through the transition from a tribe to a city, some of them alone, others in groups (the reactions are different in each case). I have also known sedentary villages in which the traditions of the nomadic encampment survived, and semi-nomadic societies that preserved them still better. Finally, I have come into contact with a few families in the northern Sahara (Zab Chergui), in the south (Ahaggar, Aïr), and in the west (Mauritania) that practised nomadism with pride.

The newcomer to the city does not, from one day to the next, become a liberal, cultivated townsman capable of acting as an individual. So the city will inevitably offend him in a number of ways. Real or imaginary, these will wound him in the most basic, the innermost, the deepest part of his personality. The 'bourgeoisified Bedouin', deprived of the protection of the great empty deserts and the unconditional support of his cousins/brothers, will henceforth fall back upon all the surrogates of protection that his means and imagination offer him: window-bars, complicated locks, fierce dogs, eunuchs...and the veil.

For country tribes do not disinherit women in order to palliate absence of the veil; the very reverse is undoubtedly the case. The veil and harem of the towns, far from being models to which the man of the countryside is bold enough to aspire, seem on the contrary pale substitutes, imitations daubed with snobbery,[8] through which the town bourgeois seeks to reconstitute a noble solitude, an imaginary world where one lives among one's kinsfolk. This man's soul is thus the tilting-ground, the lists, the bloodstained arena of a combat. In him, a type of personality that may be termed 'Bedouin' or even 'savage'—but equally well 'noble'—is struggling to survive the deadly promiscuities that settling in the city brings. To elude the inevitable conflict, he has hung a veritable 'iron curtain' between male society and women—in practice, that is, between

---

8. Snobbery is probably a response to the anguish engendered among most town-dwellers by the need to exist as an individual: the men who are least 'snobbish', least anguished, most sure of themselves, and most inwardly content are the last true warrior nomads.

city and family. He will still not succeed in satisfying the requirements of the old savage clan, but he will succeed in preserving
them—in preserving them unsated.

In this perspective, a phrase attributed to the Prophet which
orientalists of the old school were very fond of quoting is clarified:
'It [the plough] will not enter a family's dwelling without God caus-
ing abasement to enter [also] .'[9] Whether this phrase is explained
(as it is classically) in terms of the humiliation of having to submit
to a central power, or (as I am seeking to do) in terms of the
humiliation of accepting a sedentary life and hence neighbours, in
either case the reference is to the painful sensitivity of the most ancient Mediterranean society. But this phrase, so consonant with
Arab tradition, is in contradiction with everything we know of the
prophet Muhammad's doctrine. For as we have seen, he strove in
the most unceremonious and persistent manner to overturn the 'old
structures' that find expression here.[10]

The Local Bigshot *Cha-t-Diya*:
Neither the Worst Sheep Nor the Best

To give the lie to sociologists, however, there are societies in the
Maghreb in which the plough has not destroyed lineages. Sedentary
or semi-settled peasants may be seen there, rooted to the soil since
the earliest antiquity, whose degree of freedom from 'intermingling' seems to correspond to the length of time they have been settled. Among these old homesteaders, the land-register resembles a
genealogy and the layout of the graveyard is a reproduction in
miniature of the land-register. There—thanks to measures that con-
sist essentially in disinheriting all women[11]—people still live among
their kinsfolk, despite the honour-destroying plough. We may note
that this preservation of lineages among sedentary agriculturists

---

9. El Bokhari, *L'authentique tradition Musulmane:* 'The sense is that the
agriculturist, rooted to the soil, is compelled to suffer the demands of the central
power, hence in particular to pay the taxes that the nomad can escape by moving
elsewhere' (note by the translator, G.-H. Bousquet).

10. In chapter 7 above.

11. In Morocco these have not been modified since independence; I do not know
what the situation is in present-day Kabylia.

goes together with a debasement of the female condition, which here reaches one of its lowest troughs.

We know another: the suburb. This too is a transitional zone. Between the two opposed societies, conjoined despite their differences, there used to stretch—and still stretch—zones of contact. There the necessities of the one (urban life) and the compulsions of the other (the tribe) make themselves felt simultaneously. It is here, in these intermediate zones, that the greatest damage will be caused. Not in the traditional endogamous society, where marriage is *really* an affair between cousins; not in the intellectual society of the town, where the notion of 'human individual' has achieved some substance: but at every level lying between the two.[12]

Moors wittily dub the local bigshot *cha-t-diya*, a term one may attempt to translate as 'penalty sheep', since the *diya* sheep is the one you slaughter when you pay a blood-debt. For such an offering, made against your will, you take care not to choose the finest animal in the flock; but you do not dare take the worst either. The *cha-t-diya* bigshot is a good enough sheep to hope for respect, but not good enough to be sure of getting it, whence the zeal he displays when his prestige is in question. He, more than anyone else, will make a great show of piety and hermetically seal away his daughters and wives.

In France, we have known similar cases of painful ascent matched with pretension. In the seventeenth century, the *Bourgeois Gentilhomme* ('Cit Turned Gentleman') was laughed at by the Court. At the beginning of the twentieth, it was bourgeois intellectuals of the Third Republic who used the term *primaire* ('elementary') to denote a man full of himself but with little culture, who thanks to some superficial, ill-digested reading has an answer for everything. Such individuals really existed, at a time when compulsory elementary schooling was delivering a mortal blow to our old peasant civilization. And during that period an intelligent illiterate, possess-

---

12. In our day, the sedentarization of nomads in fact produces the same result as urbanization, in other words social disintegration; but nowadays good land is scarce and widely scattered. In very ancient sedentary societies (in Kabylia, for example), one finds 'old structures' that have resisted sedentarization, perhaps because of their very early establishment. It is also possible that 'old structures' that have been destroyed tend to reconstitute themselves, given time and means.

ing the traditional culture of our country areas, was more interesting, wiser, and more 'refined' than his son, whom seven years of elementary education had untaught one civilization without giving him full access to another. But the grandson has now taken his revenge, so that today the social category in question is no longer encountered. Of course, vulgarity, self-importance, and lack of social 'polish' are still on display. But among us these failings are limited to individuals, and have ceased to be a caste phenomenon, whereas the *cha-t-diya* still flourishes in the villages and suburbs of Africa.

More Veiled Women in the Villages, Fewer in the Towns

The phenomenon of invisible, continuous erosion of life, which has always undermined urban centres, has been halted nowadays in the cities by the medical advances of our century. Thanks to this, individualism is becoming generalized in a certain milieu, and one may even hope that civic sense—which is already appearing among a few citizens—will likewise have a chance to assert itself there. But the numerical advantage still lies with the men of the past, since during this period the rural exodus has further escalated and peasants are invading the suburbs and shanty towns by their thousands. The two phenomena have opposite results: on the one hand, town-dwellers are becoming citizens, to the greatest advantage of their country; on the other, we see haughty nomads, proud landowners, becoming 'vagrants'.[13]

Simultaneous with these two great phenomena, we can observe a small indication: a shift in the wearing of the veil. The European public, which travels increasingly to the cities of the East but is less familiar with the countryside, thinks that use of the veil is now dwindling throughout the Muslim world. In reality, it is dwindling in certain milieux and increasing in others. It is indeed dwindling in the cities, where at the beginning of this century it was still universal, and this is something every tourist can see. In the countryside, however, where it was unknown twenty years ago, it is on the rise. In Moroccan, Algerian, Tunisian, or Libyan villages (to speak only of regions I have visited recently), I have seen for myself that *it is*

---

13. Except in Mauritania, where the last happy nomads of the Maghreb live.

now adopted, on an everyday basis, by women whose mothers did not veil themselves.

In his excellent study of 'regroupment centres' in Kabylia, Pierre Bourdieu noted: 'Another sign of how the style of social relations has been transformed: the appearance of the veil for women. In the rural society of former times, women who did not have to hide themselves from members of their clan, were obliged when they went to the spring (or secondarily to the fields) to follow side routes, at traditionally fixed hours: thus sheltered from alien eyes, they did not wear the veil and had no knowledge of...an existence cloistered within the house. In the regroupment centre, as in the city, there is no longer any separate space for each social unit: the male space and the female space overlap. In the end, moreover, the partial or total abandonment of agricultural labour condemns men to remain all day long in the village streets or at home. It is thus out of the question for women to be able to leave the house freely, without drawing scorn and dishonour upon the men of the family. The peasant woman transplanted into the city, unable to adopt the townswoman's veil without repudiating herself as a country-woman, had to avoid so much as appearing on her own doorstep. By creating a social environment of the urban type, the regroupment centre leads to the appearance of the veil, which allows movement among strangers.'[14]

Can it be argued that the veil, among other indications, thus represents entry into the bourgeoisie, and hence, in European eyes, a rise on the social ladder? But this conception is precisely not that of the Maghreb, where for centuries the 'swell' was the nomad, the Bedouin. Furthermore, on the social rung immediately above, the middle-class woman who becomes a great lady nowadays often signals this advance by discarding her veil. If you wanted to joke about it, you could compare this female evolution to the seemingly analogous case of a man I knew from the Aurès: he began as a cook, drinking anisette; he then became a prosperous Algiers merchant, in public consuming only mineral water; finally, once on the

14. Pierre Bourdieu, *Le déracinement. La crise de l'agriculture traditionelle en Algérie*, Paris 1964, p. 132.

way to becoming an international personality, he began to accept the whisky that corresponded to his 'rating'.

A Case of Social Urticaria

Female inheritance, just like urbanization, as we have seen effectively 'pulverizes' tribal society. The latter, therefore, defends itself as best it can: in other words, by secluding its daughters strictly, in order to marry them to cousins all the same. It is important to remember these three phases of the inner conflict of Mediterranean society: first a *compulsion*, whose origins are neolithic, to live among one's own kinsfolk; then a *frustration of this compulsion* (which also goes back a very long way, since it is just a fraction older than the oldest historical document), so that alien neighbours must be tolerated; finally a *demographic mechanism*, which has allowed this ancient conflict to remain active from prehistory to our own day.

Normally, in fact, a thwarted mechanism will eventually break down, in one way or another. In other words, if a motor runs with the brake on for long, either the motor will smash the brake or the brake will smash the motor. It is, therefore, curious to find that south of the Mediterranean structures that have failed to adapt have nevertheless survived almost indefinitely. The phenomenon occurs at the point of contact between two societies: the urban and the tribal. These two societies coexist side by side all round the Mediterranean, mutually opposed, but conjoined. And until the last ten years it was tribal society, 'the society of cousins', that penetrated urban society, national society, the society of citizens, *not the other way round.*

As we have seen, this does not mean that endogamy corresponds naturally to a debasement of the female condition. Indeed, it is even likely that marriage between cousins represented a step forward in this domain. For in a truly endogamous tribe, the woman who marries a quasi-brother for whom she had been destined from birth enjoys considerable respect and affection (this is so much the case that the appellation 'cousin' used by a husband speaking to his wife is always felt to express respect and love). Exogamy, for its part, can cause damage by separating the young girl cruelly from the only surroundings she knows, and by making her into an 'article of exchange'. The debasement of women thus accompanies not endogamy, but an *unfinished* evolution of endogamous society—unfinished because of the ceaseless resuscitation of tribal ideas and prejudices in the heart of the great urban civilizations of the Orient. In this second half of the twentieth century, the new factor is thus not the conflict but its evolution.

The situation has in fact been changing for fifty years, in the sense that people now have better life-chances in the cities of the Orient than in the countryside.[15] (I say 'life-chances' and not 'birth-chances': the latter, by contrast, are growing somewhat smaller, at least in the *urban* heart of the big cities.[16]) The result, in the towns, is to maintain the ancient equilibrium described in this chapter without any significant change. As in the past, the weight of numbers continues in fact to lie with the rural mass: 'neolithic', fast-breeding, wanting in civic virtues. In other words, with the Republic of Cousins. As in the past, this human mass continues to crush and submerge an intellectual elite which, however clear-sighted, is still too few in numbers to win dominance. However, there is education, which might reverse the flow one day.

The only real change is that this urban elite is not decimated to the same extent as in the past.[17] It is increasingly aware, increasingly well-informed, and increasingly exasperated by the conflict that pits it against the rural masses. Among the latter, birth-chances are as great as the life on offer is tragically deprived. Deeply unsettled by poverty and the exoduses it provokes, and by an inadequate 'scattering' of schools, it is 'detribalized' without being able to

---

15. One obvious reason for this reversal is related to the presence of doctors in the towns of Africa and Asia, and to their tragic absence in the countryside of those continents. But there is another, less obvious one: the distribution of modern poverty. In the cities of the East, the very poor sometimes find a job, state aid, crumbs from the wealthy, whereas in the over-populated countryside famine is nowadays becoming a scourge from which there is neither refuge nor escape.

16. In asserting this, I am basing myself mainly on ethnography of the old school (studies unsupported by figures): a great many statistics, in fact, confuse 'life expectancy' with 'birth expectancy' and make no distinction, in the town, between the long-standing resident and the newcomer. Among long-established town-dwellers, concern to raise children properly has reduced the birth-rate somewhat.

17. At least by disease. It is, however, still decimated by emigration; the elite of the under-developed countries takes refuge in the industrial countries.

achieve any conception of—or respect for—the individual being. The great victim of this situation, of course, is woman, who ceases to be a 'cousin' but is not yet a 'person'.

This means it is quite unrealistic to hope that things will sort themselves out in this key domain, if matters merely take their course. Only a continuous intervention by the Muslim governments of an extremely energetic—and not very popular—kind could compensate for the numerical weighting that currently favours archaic ways in their countries. But everything hangs together in a society: everything moves forward or everything stagnates. And in a world moving as fast as ours, to stagnate is fatal.

9
Women and the Veil[1]

The Last 'Colony'

When the first trembling of the modern ebullition began to ruffle the surface of the deep human sea known as 'Afro-Asian', it was no accident that the female veil became a symbol: a symbol of the enslavement of half the human race. In our age of generalized decolonization, the vast world of women indeed remains a colony in many respects. Widely plundered despite legislation, sometimes sold,[2] often beaten, coerced into forced labour, murdered almost with impunity[3], the Mediterranean woman is among today's serfs.

Yet the disadvantages of this alienation are well known to all sociologists (UNESCO is currently showing concern), and to most magistrates. For both are aware that it lowers the active potential of the nation and consequently weakens the State; that it paralyses all forms of collective and individual evolution, male as much as female, and consequently slows down or curbs progress; and that it cause multiple and irreparable injuries to children, and hence to the future. As for man, the supposed author and apparent beneficiary

---

1. Part of this chapter was published in *Mélanges offerts à Charles-André Julien*, Paris 1964.

2. This is not a reference to the marriage-portion, which by Islamic law the future husband has to hand over to his wife before he can marry her. Indeed, the marriage-portion is a safeguard provided for the wife, since in the event of widowhood or divorce it must remain hers. It refers rather to actual sale, unfortunately more and more common in the poor suburbs, though exceptional in religious areas and always considered shameful.

3. When a wife is suspected of adultery, the husband, father, or brother who murders her is automatically acquitted by public opinion in all countries of (or influenced by) the Mediterranean. That is why Italian lawmakers had to fix a

of this repression, at every period of his life—as child, as husband, as father—he is a direct victim of it; and the weight of bitterness that falls to his lot as a result is sometimes not very different from that which crushes his female companion.

'Whosoever Removes the Head-Dress or Kerchief... Shall Incur the Penalty'

The traveller who ranges through the Mediterranean fringe of Christianity—Spain, the south of France, Corsica, Italy, Sicily, Sardinia, Greece, Cyprus, Christian Lebanon—encounters no detail of costume so strikingly eye-catching as the veil of Muslim women. But a few characteristic features deserving of attention can still be observed. On the Christian shores of the Mediterranean, one may follow the zigzag path of an invisible frontier. Outside it, couples walk together on Sundays and frequent the same shops; in her own village, a woman accompanied by a member of her family will dare to consume an innocent drink in a café; a peasant woman of more than thirty-five may appear in public without wearing a black shawl over her head. On the inner side of this frontier, men walk the street alone; they go alone to the bars; and a woman's presence in a café—even in the company of a near relative—to this day appears as unusual as it would in Baghdad.[4]

Thus on the Gargano peninsula (spur of the Italian boot) some of the villages are actually reminiscent of the layout of Kabyle settlements, in the way they are adapted architecturally to separation of the sexes. During the teeming rush-hours which, in summer, correspond to the end of the siesta, the passer-by on the squares and main

---

minimum of three years imprisonment to punish such crimes. So far as I know, in the Mediterranean countries (or those influenced by the Mediterranean like the American south-west or Latin America), when such a minimum is not imposed by the law, acquittal is the rule. In England, by contrast, and in North America generally, the husband who murders his wife is liable to suffer the maximum penalty.

4. Dominique Fernandez (*The Mother Sea*, p. 23) notes the same phenomenon on the west coast: 'We had already noticed, during our journey from the frontier to Naples, that one very rarely meets a couple in Italy. If we happened to catch sight of a man and a woman alone in a restaurant, they were invariably sitting opposite each other without speaking, as if they had nothing to say to each other. Most often, we saw whole groups of men and women—ten or twelve to a table, as protection against the dreaded tête-à-tête. And at night, in bars, men only.'

streets will make his way through male-only crowds, tirelessly spewed forth by the forbidding little doors of the old houses; and the shops, cafés, and public gardens are filled with men, and men alone. If, on the other hand, chance or curiosity leads someone into less easily accessible alley-ways at the same hour, he will be able to rub shoulders with an equally dense mass of humanity, but this time one that is exclusively female, in which the only virile elements are small males under eight clutching their mothers' aprons.

In Ragusa, Sicily, out of thirty housewives questioned, only three said they went out to do their shopping, and this was solely because they were forced to do so, because their husbands were dead or sick.[5]

In southern Italy (the province of Potenza, ancient Lucania), Dominique Fernandez notes in connection with nuptial defloration: 'The newly-weds, meanwhile, at grips with the enemy within, their ancient inhibitions, try to triumph over the night and their fear and to be ready for the visit of inspection promised by the bride's mother-in-law for the following morning.'[6]

In Greece too, especially in Thessaly, mothers-in-law remain true to the custom that requires that bedclothes be exposed at a window on the morning after a wedding, supposedly proving the virginity of their new daughters-in-law to other local matrons.

In southern France (including Corsica), compulsory education, urban influences, and intercourse with a northern civilization have brought about a partial disappearance of these customs, so that it is necessary to go back a century or two to find them flourishing. But here, at any rate, is an example: 'Whosoever removes the head-dress or kerchief [covering a woman's hair]; or to use the vulgar expression 'attaches'; or , whether by public or private threats or by any other violent means, prevents a young girl or a widow from marrying, shall incur the penalty.' This provision can be found in a sort of code promulgated under Paoli's government, in the month of May 1766. In Corsica at that time, if someone wanted to prevent a girl from marrying he uncovered her head in public,[7] for after

---

5. Quoted by R. Rochefort, *Le travail en Sicile*, Paris 1916, p. 86.
6. Fernandez, p. 82.
7. See too p. 108 above.

such an affront only the perpetrator of the assault could, without shame, marry the woman who had been its victim. Before the wedding, however, he stood an excellent chance of being killed by his future in-laws.

Analogies between Christian customs and those generally attributed only to Muslim society are not confined to such anodine likenesses. In our own day, in the Greek countryside a wife *suspected* of adultery must be sent back by her husband to her family, where in the name of honour her own father or elder brother *must* kill her, usually with a knife. If she has no father or brother, the village will expect an uncle or even a first cousin to undertake the bloody rite. All this still goes on (my information, which comes from a Greek statesman, dates from 1964). The murder of a girl by her brother was customary in Italy,[8] and may still sometimes be encountered there. It remains common in Lebanon. In Muslim countries, I know of examples in Morocco and in Kabylia, but not in the Aurès, not in Mauritania, and not in Tuareg territory. In Iraq, it is accepted by public opinion and treated lightly by the law.[9]

For our own part, interpreting these stories in the light of the Mediterranean context, we shall explain this obligation to have her closest kinsman punish a wife's adultery by the rule of the *vendetta*. For otherwise the woman's family would have the right to exact vengeance upon a murdering husband. It is also the vendetta that explains the putting to death of an adulterous wife by stoning, a custom still widely practised in the Mediterranean basin.[10] Everything proceeds as if a woman's adultery were a crime against the society to which she belongs, and not just the breach of a private commitment. So the society wreaks vengeance. But it wreaks vengeance in such a way that responsibility for the crime is shared among all its individual members, so that no one of them has to answer for it personally.

---

8. See pp. 98–9 above.
9. See note 13, chapter 5.
10. An Algerian friend of mine witnessed the stoning in Mecca a few years ago of a young man and woman who had confessed their amorous relations. In a village south of Sétif, when an unmarried girl had a child in 1959 and her family failed to react, it was the village that stoned her; the child survived, contrary to custom.

An informed observer of Italy writes, in connection with the education of girls and boys: 'We shall not come back to the girls, brought up with the idea that the only important thing in life is their virginity. There is nothing astonishing in their not bothering to develop their minds or affirm their personalities. They know that their most precious quality does not really belong to them, that their husband will take it away in one stroke and that afterwards they will be worthless. All their lives will have been played out in a few minutes, once and for all, often before they have even grown out of childhood. Half of the population is in this way prevented from exercising the slightest influence on the intellectual and moral evolution of the South. As for the boys, things are hardly better. Worshipped as gods from their cradle days, surrounded by a swarm of women ready to satisfy their whims, never subjected to a time-table, never punished or rewarded systematically but allowed to do as they please.... they reach manhood as unprepared as newly-born babies. At twenty or twenty-five, the encounter with real life... becomes for them a dreadful catastrophe.'[11] And the same observer points out: 'After ninety years of federation, in 1950, revenue per head of population in the North was twice that in the South; today, after more than ten years of economic "miracle", revenue per head in Milan is four times greater than in Calabria or Sicily.'[12]

All this hangs together inexorably. For if the men keep the women in this debased situation, it is the women who have brought up little boys and passed on to them anew the old prehistoric viruses. Crushed women manufacture vain, irresponsible manikins, and together they constitute the props of a society whose units steadily grow in number but diminish in quality. Yet courage, intelligence, all the great and rare human virtues, are distributed among them at exactly the same rate as among the peoples of the North, but *something* supervenes to stifle them. This 'something' is, in particular, the social constraint that imposes on a father or brother the barbarous modes of conduct of which we have just seen examples, sometimes upon mere suspicion. As for the nature and

11. Fernandez, pp. 53–4.
12. Ibid., p. 45.

origins of that constraint, it has precisely been one of the subjects of this book.

On the Sea's Muslim Shore

South of the Mediterranean, the veil no longer hides only the hair, but the entire face.[13] It does not constitute merely a picturesque and somewhat anachronistic item of dress, but a real boundary. On one side of this boundary there lives and progresses a national society—which, therefore, turns out to be a half-society. On the other side, women—ignorant and ignored—stagnate. At the beginning of this century, throughout north Africa and the immense reaches of western Asia, the rule allowed of no exception: all women in towns—apart from a few old servants—hid their faces beneath an all-enveloping cowl whenever they were obliged to leave the harem. Women in towns, but not women in the countryside: for the latter always used to go about with their faces uncovered in olden days.

In our own time, in the streets of Turkish or Iranian towns, the tourist still sometimes passes a woman whose face is concealed behind thick, dark cloth: but rarely, since in these two countries, well before the Second World War, two vigorous military men become heads of state forbade the practice, and accompanied the prohibition with harsh penalties.[14] In Iraq, in 1961, one saw very few women in the streets, but these were not all veiled. In Lebanon at the same date in the main arteries of the big cities I noticed cer-

---

13. 'The Greek wife who shows her face at the front-window of her house is committing a breach of conjugal fidelity which, in her husband's eyes, is worthy of divorce.' Aristophanes, *Thesmophoriazusae*, lines 797–801. 'It is likewise a breach of conjugal fidelity for the Roman wife of the sixth century from the foundation of Rome (second century BC) to go out of her house without her husband's knowledge or to show her uncovered face in public.' (Plautus, Mercator, Act IV, Scene 5). See Pierre Noailles, 'Les tabous du marriage dans le droit primitif des romains', *Annales Sociologiques* C, part 2, p. 25.
14. Mustafa Kemal Pasha, first president of the Turkish republic (elected 1923, died 1938), and Reza Shah Pahlavi (elected king of Iran in 1925, died in 1944). These two heads of state, both former soldiers, imposed sanctions to eliminate the veil and more or less succeeded, provisionally. Forty years later, Iranians asked whether they preferred the current emperor to his father replied: 'Yes, because he has allowed the veil to be worn again.'

tain elegant women who, though frequently dressed in suits of the most modern cut, also wore a miniature black hat-veil; in big villages in the south, the veil was still very widespread. In Egypt, Syria, Jordan, and West Pakistan—countries I also visited in 1961—I noticed the presence of a few veiled women in luxury districts, but the veil remained common in the poor suburbs. Four years later, in 1965, my Syrian and Egyptian friends told me that it had become almost exceptional. In short, Saudi Arabia, Yemen, and Afghanistan are the only Muslim states of any importance in the Arab East today where women in the towns are still as confined, as masked, and as closely watched as their grandmothers were.

In Morocco, on the other hand, despite the efforts of King Muhammad V, the veil still remains very widespread. Yet there too girls in secondary or higher education and some young wives have stopped wearing it, and scarcely any longer encounter hostility. In Lybia (Tripoli or Benghazi), the same tendency may be observed. In Tunisia, the veil is on the way out: its disappearance corresponds to a deeper evolution, the credit for which must largely be attributed to President Bourguiba.[15]

Algeria, where during the Seven Year War the veil played various strategic roles, is still going through a process of self-examination. Its revolution was clearly the work of modernist, not retrograde elements, but when its cadres left the underground, they lost strength heavily and came to feel the weight of the masses who had

---

15. Habib Bourguiba, *La femme, élément de progrès dans la société*, Monastir 1965: 'When still a young child...I told myself that if one day I had the power to do so, I would make haste to redress the wrong done to women' (p. 7). 'In my family, and from contact with my mother and grandmother, I clearly saw the unjust and wretched destiny imposed on women....Despite all their efforts and all their merits, women remained inferior beings and people used wounding terms to describe them. I suffered in my innermost heart from this injustice...men had to take their distance from women and behave like masters' (p. 6). 'Other customs have been revealed to me in these past few days which have surprised and deeply disturbed me. At Djerba, a young school prefect of twenty-one was to marry an official. According to custom, the future bride was shut up in an underground cell, smeared with clay to lighten her complexion, and crammed with noodles to fatten her' (p. 23). 'Another equally serious case has come to my knowledge....This involved an old hawker from the Berka market who was owed two hundred and fifty dinars by a father, and who...intended to get an educated girl in payment' (p. 24). (The girl had gone to her headmistress to ask for work, in order, she said, to pay off one of her father's creditors.)

followed them. In any case, the facts are there: to everyone's surprise, the towns of Algeria are still to be reckoned among those
Muslim cities where veiled women are encountered in large
numbers, while in its villages too the female veil—and everything it
symbolizes—is gaining ground.
We should not be too quick to speak of regression. For Algeria is
a young country and the weight of numbers currently resides with
boys under twenty, most of whom, because of the war, have been
raised by their mothers. Now Algerian mothers consider it their duty to beat their daughters, in order to accustom them to submission. But they *never* oppose their sons. This kind of upbringing
does not necessarily produce delinquents, at least in the countryside. In big cities and crowded suburbs, however, in combination with examples from the street and an absence of fathers, it has
engendered the results one might have expected. It is thus to avoid
the ribaldries of urchins that women have taken once more to the
veil in many Algerian towns.
It is also worth noting that if one meets large numbers of veiled
women in the streets of Algiers, this is because they leave their
houses more than other Mediterranean women, whether for shopping, visits, or jobs. This economic and technical participation they
are beginning to exercise in the life of the country is an index of
progress, for themselves and for their nation. Further signs of
social evolution: in Algerian towns, one more and more often
meets 'modern' young couples, who live alone and devote themselves to their children's upbringing, between the refrigerator and
television, which consecrate their intimacy. At the same time, the
custom of the honeymoon is becoming common among public
employees and in the liberal professions.
During the sumptuous feasts still customarily given on the occasion of a wedding, one may now see young men and women danc-
ing the twist, the madison, or the cha-cha-cha together, under
heavily shaded lights. The astonished foreigner will think in terms
of 'modernism', but this time wrongly. The cha-cha-cha apart, we
are in fact enveloped in tradition here. For anyone taking the trouble to find out will soon perceive that the only males admitted to
these revelries are the everlasting cousins of the great Mediterranean valley, for whom the gynaeceum of the Maghreb has always

been half-open. The degrees of tolerance actually distinguish between two families, not between two epochs.

The Ancient World, Beyond the Maghreb

This study is devoted not to a Muslim phenomenon, but to the explanation of one that is far vaster, since it characterizes the geographical zone in which, after the neolithic discoveries, there was disseminated a family structure, at once optimistic and fierce, that is still our own (give or take a few nuances). Mainly for lack of first-hand information, the book unfortunately leaves aside the countries of Far Eastern Islam, which had great piety in common and underwent Mediterranean influences through the medium of their faith. But our aim has been to unearth customs far older than the Muslim faith, and to determine their limits.

In Africa, these go far beyond those of the Maghreb or of the white race.[16] Vincent Monteil, who has explored all the points of convergence between 'Darkest Africa' and Islam with far-sighted attention to detail, wrote in 1964: 'The seclusion of women is an exceptional occurrence in Black Africa, outside the families of marabouts. Exceptions to this rule are reported, however, among Fulani sedentary agriculturists....But Hausa husbands in Nigeria do not allow their wives to go out, and in towns simply keep them shut up: total isolation....is considered preferable to a "blind man's marriage".'[17] Here too evolution is a two-way process, and among the Yoruba in Ibadan, in western Nigeria, a brand-new Muslim sect of Gandele veils and secludes its women—a new phenomenon, observed on the spot by Vincent Monteil in April 1965.

The Influence of Invisible Women

In urban centres (meaning the sum of families settled in any city for several generations), many people are currently evolving towards respect for the human individual, even when this individual is a woman. Unfortunately, however, the numerical advantage still lies

---

16. The neolithic in Senegal goes back some six thousand years, dating from a little later than that of North Africa.
17. Monteil, *L'Islam noir*, p. 172.

with the rural masses flooding more than ever into the towns. Apart from their deprivations, so difficult to remedy, they bring with them an almost crushing weight of prehistoric prejudices.

In the hybrid milieu—half rural, half urban—which is currently tending to submerge all others, woman's influence, precisely because of her 'occultation', remains great, even too great. Children are strongly influenced by their mothers in all countries, but the children of veiled women more than others, because their mothers raise them alone during their early, most important, years.[18] Moreover, the mother belongs to the child so totally that the bond never unravels, and the child finds itself dangerously enslaved by this possession. So it may easily be imagined how a mechanism whose twofold result is to exaggerate the influence of mothers upon their children while simultaneously depriving women in general of normal relations with life, society, the nation, and progress, can—during periods when evolution is rapid—engender the most pernicious consequences.

The young woman, for her part, has to accustom herself from childhood to the annihilation of her personality and, to that end, suffer ceaseless though unavailing bullying: Mediterranean women have as much personality as anyone else, and the bullying far from softening their character, sours it. That is not all. As a result of the territorial dislocation of the clan, peasant women are more and more often induced to marry an outsider, hence a stranger. So they not only have to separate for ever from the happy, fraternal band with which they have been brought up, but must also win acceptance from a group of a priori hostile women. Here is where the worst of female situations awaits them. They first undergo a terrible period of adjustment to new surroundings. It is true during this time they may sometimes be lucky enough to be sustained by their

---

18. In the Maghreb today, children's relations with their parents may be reversed in some circles where the father has undergone modern influences while the mother has remained enclosed in an archaic world: the result is no better. I have known families in which the father, an educated man, was led by love and solicitude to take the mother's place in the upbringing of very young children: the consequences of this literal 'inversion' can be psychologically dramatic, ranging from simple nervous depression to attempted suicide by the eldest son, obsessed by his own sense of responsibility.

husbands' love: but the almost inevitable result of this love is to increase the jealous hostility of the female milieu towards them, a hostility all the greater in that the new wife often occupies a place for which she was not destined, thus ousting some niece or beloved cousin.

If the young wife becomes a mother, maternal love will make her more ingenious in pleasing others, and give her courage to bear the harassments with which the women of her husband's clan beset her—for a divorce would separate her mercilessly from her children. Her in-laws, for their part, will be grateful to her after a time 'for bringing little ones'. For these reasons, the couple sometimes endures. Time then passes, the wheel turns, and the day comes when, thanks to her sons, it is the turn of the wife—now grown old—to indulge her whims. She then torments her young daughters-in-law horribly, and traditionally constitutes the firmest bastion of the ancient idiocies.[19] But by now even this belated happiness of hers is disputed; for a new world, where she knows she has no kind of place, is everywhere imposing its claims.

Amid female storms, most men resort to empiricism. They entrust their mothers with full authority, the larder keys, and the money; then bring their wives—often on the sly, and depending on their means and the opportunity—a dress, a piece of jewellery, a cake of perfumed soap. When they fail to appease either one, they are left, as everywhere, with the solution of taking refuge in the café. After a few failures, they grow weary and divorce, sometimes not without regret.

In this phase of evolution, all family situations, at all stages of life, now bristle with thorns, imposing on every man and every woman an obsession with flight: forward flight into the future for some, flight into the past for all the rest. In the multifarious political and economic difficulties of the present, this underlying secret dissatisfaction still seeps through in every life. So it is quite comprehensible that the endogamous tribe, the Republic of Cousins—at once alive in people's memories and inaccessible, an image, myth, and model—should appear a haven of peace, understanding, virtue, and happiness: a golden age. But it is not possible

---

19. This means that in Muslim countries 'feminism' is a male affair.

to go backward, and all the efforts expended in that direction have only one result: to halt progress, obstruct the future, and hold society at the most painful and dangerous stage of its evolution.

Index

Abraham, 68, 69, 70
Alexander the Great, 67
Alimen, Henriette, 77n., 79n., 81n.
Amenophis III, 65
Amenophis IV, 65, 66 and n.
Ammon, 68
Ankhsenpaton, 66
Antigone, 16
Aref, General, 98n.
Aristophanes, 171n.
Arsinoe, 67
Auboyer, J., 73n.
Averroès, 116, 126, 129, 147n., 151
Ay, 66
Aymard, A., 73n.

Barrère, Guy, 86n., 88n.
Barth, J., 55n.
Baudelaire, Charles, 109
Beaumont, Pierre de, 130n.
Ben-Ammi, 69
Bernot, L., 21n.
Bernus, Edmond, 118n.
Berque, Jacques, 104 and n., 115n.
Bichat, Xavier, 24 and n.
Blackman, W.S., 25n., 82n.
Blancard, R., 21n.
Bloch, Marc, 129n.
Boas, Franz, 40n.
Boucheman, Albert de, 128n
Bourdieu, Pierre, 21n., 162 and n.
Bourguiba, Habib, 172 and n.
Braudel, Fernand, 12n.
Breteau, Claude and Mabrouka,
    100n.
Busquet, J., 108n.

Caesar, Julius, 129
Cardine, Don Leonardo del, 99
Charlemagne, 139
Childe, V. Gordon, 42n., 50 and n.,
    53n., 57, 82n.
Chombart de Lauwe, P.-H., 140n.
Christ, see Jesus
Christopher, Saint, 88n.
Cid Campeador (Rodrigo Diaz), 103
Cleopatras, the, 67-8
Clothru, 71
Cohen, Marcel, 33n.
Collignon, M., 90n.
Columbus, Christopher, 52
Conchobhar, 71
Condominas, Georges, 63 and n.
Coon, Carleton C., 47n.
Coppens, J., 39n.
Coulanges, Fustel de, 129n.
Croce, Benedetto, 98n.
Cúchulainn, 71
Cuisinier, Jeanne, 34n.
Czarnowski, Stefan, 58n., 59n., 71n.

Daninos, Pierre, 151n.
David, 68
Dawood, N.J., 142
Deirdriu, 71
Desroches-Noblecourt,
    Christiane, 65n.
Dionysius the Younger, 71
Dionysius the Elder, 70-71
Drioton, Étienne, 81n.
Duveyrier, C., 55n.

El Bokhari, 87n., 159n.

Engels, Friedrich, 48n.
Esau, 69

Febvre, Lucien, 70n., 75n.
Feilberg, C.-G., 85n.
Fernandez, Dominique, 98n., 99,
    167n., 168 and n., 170 and n.
Ferrante, Don (Conte d'Aliffe), 99
Fleming, Alexander, 56
Forde, D., 58n.
Fortes, Meyer, 58 and n.
Fourastié, Jean, 50n.
Franco, General, 139
François I, 98

Gast, Marceau, 85n., 118n.
Génicot, Léopold, 130n.
Gennep, Arnold van, 107 and n.
Geoffroy, Auguste, 79n.
Germi, Pietro, 103
Gernet, Louis, 66n., 70 and n.
Goux, Jean-Michel, 72n., 107n.
Griaule, Marcel, 21 and n.
Guillaume le Testu, 88

Hanoteaux, D., 119n.
Henri IV, 52
Heredia, José-Maria de, 112
Herodotus, 13, 81–92 passim, 93
Hewes, G.W., 12n.
Horace, 16
Hubert, Henri, 58n., 59n., 71n.,
    119 and n.

Isaac, 69
Isis, 73n.

Jacob, 69, 70 and n.
Jacquemont, N., 75n.
Jesus, 59n., 136, 141n., 142n.
Joan of Arc, 139
Jouin, Jeanne, 86 and n.
Julien, Charles-André, 166n.

Kemal, Mustafa, 171n.
Kenyon, K., 50n.
Khaldun, Ibn, 90, 116, 125 and n.,
    126 and n., 129, 147n., 151
Kluckhohn, Clyde, 40n., 43n., 50

Laban, 70 and n.
La Blache, Vidal de, 53
Laoust, Émile, 85n.
Leah, 70 and n.
Le Coeur, Charles, 85n.
Leroi-Gourhan, André, 38n., 42
    and n.
Letourneux, H., 119n.
Lévi-Strauss, Claude, 36n., 37, 44n.,
    55n., 58, 59n., 62 and n., 76n.
Levy, Claude, 72n.
Lot, 68

Mâle, Émile, 88n.
Man, E.-H., 59n.
Mandeville, Jean de, 88n.
Marcy, Georges, 85n., 146n.
Mauss, Marcel, 55n., 58n., 138–9
Mead, Margaret, 16, 55n., 76 and n.
Medhbh (Mab), 71
Meritaton, 65
Moab, 69
Moch, Jules, 23n.
Mohammed V, 172
Monteil, Vincent, 126n., 133n., 174
    and n.
Morra, Isabella, 98–9
Morton, Frederic, 105n.
Moses, 136
Muhammad, 82, 83, 136, 159
Musset, Alfred de, 109

Napoleon, 140
Nefertiti, 65, 66
Nicolaisen, Johannes, 134n., 146n.,
    147n.
Nicolas, Francis, 64 and n.
Noailles, Pierre, 54n.
Nougier, Louis-René, 51n.
Nouschi, A., 80 and n.

Odrio, Friar, 88n.
Orsini, Prince, 99
Osiris, 73n.

Pahlavi, Reza, 171n.
Paoli, Pasquale, 168
Pasteur, Louis, 56, 155, 156
Paul, Saint, 137 and n., 138 and n.

Plautus, 171n.
Pliny, 129
Pomponius Mela, 89n.
Posener, Georges, 79n.
Ptolemies, the, 67–8
Pytheas, 59n., 71

Rachel, 70 and n.
Radcliffe-Brown, A.R., 58n.
Rameses III, 25n.
Rebecca, 69
Robert the Pious, 139
Rocal, Abbé Georges, 107 and n.
Rochefort, R., 168n.
Rocher, Guy, 140n.
Rodinson, Maxime, 30n.
Romulus, 54n.
Rosenthal, Franz, 126n.
Rothschilds, the, 105 and n., 106

Sandoval de Castro, Don Diego,
    98–9
Santucci: Baptista, Lucie, Stefano,
    108
Sarah, 68
Satamon, 65

Schmidt senior, T., 55n.
Shapiro, M., 40n.
Si-Mohand-Salah, 121–5
Slane, William M. de, 126n.
Smenkhkeré, 65, 66
Snofru, 81n.
Spengler, Oswald, 157
Stendhal (Marie-Henri Beyle), 99
    and n.
Strabo, 59n., 71 and n.
Sutter, Jean, 72n., 107n.

Tacitus, 129
Tamar, 68
Tashery, 66
Thackeray, William M., 151n.
Tiye, 65, 66
Tutankhamūn, 65n., 66

Valéry, Paul, 157 and n.
Valio, Angelo Franco, 108
Vallet, Michel, 72n.
Vandier, Jacques, 81n.

Westermarck, E., 54n.
Wittfogel, Karl, 94n., 95n., 97n.

6 1981